LEFT HAND GOLFE

LEFT HANDED GOLFER

PETER SMITH

SBL Springfield Books Limited

Published by Springfield Books Limited,
Norman Road, Denby Dale,
Huddersfield, HD8 8TH, England.

© Copyright MasterClass Design Ltd, 1993.

Designed and produced by MasterClass Design Ltd,
37 Seymour Close, Birmingham B29 7JD, England.

Photographs by Mark Newcombe, Debbie Newcombe,
Ken Lewis and Peter Smith
Illustrations by MasterClass Design Studio.
Layout and Jacket design by Keith Harris.

First edition 1993.

British Library Cataloguing in Publication Data

Smith, Peter
Left Handed Golfer
  1 Title
  796.352

ISBN 1 85688 033 8

Printed and bound in Hong Kong by Colorcraft Ltd.

Contents

Introduction

Although one in ten people are left handed the ratio of left handed golfers to those playing right handed is nowhere as high as 1:10. Many left handers play golf right handed.

Many have found it difficult to find suitable left handed clubs; others, just beginning golf, have picked up the first club they were offered and begun swinging. More often than not, that club would have been made for a right handed golfer.

Golf books tend to be written for right handed players and those whose natural choice would be to play left handed have, in the past, had to reverse left and right to understand how to play the game. We have only found one other book, first published several years ago, which can be read by a left handed player without "translation".

In this book we have asked several top left handed professionals for their advice.

That advice and instruction has been freely given by the four main professionals in this book, one of whom has played golf at the highest level, playing in the 1977 Ryder Cup; one of only a few left handers ever to play in that great event. Another is currently playing on the European Tour and is the second longest driver of the golf ball in Europe; the other two are sturdy club professionals who teach almost every day of their lives, to both left and right handed players.

The valuable experience each of these professionals has is distilled and concentrated into this book, making it the perfect teaching manual for all left handed golfers.

It begins with the basics of golf, from the initial alignment of the club face to the stance and grip. It deals then with the vital short game, where every golfer, whether they can come close to matching Stuart Little's prodigious power off the tee or not, the opportunity to get the ball close to the hole to either save par or achieve a net par.

We take the fear out of bunker shots and help you to attack those other trouble shots with confidence - in amongst the trees, rough, sloping lies and playing in strong wind.

Even the longest hitters need to be able to putt once they are on the green and we have help for those who regularly fail to sink those important putts at the first attempt.

Then we come to driving, revealing the secret of extra power off the tee and in the long game.

Finally we come to strategy on the course, without which not even the best strikers of the golf ball could get round with a reasonable score. Warming up exercises and practice ground routines are explained, helping you to get the very best from your golf, and we also take a quick look at the equipment which is now on the market for left handed players.

Of course, golf is a part-time pastime for most of us so, whilst urging you to practise whenever you can if you want to improve your golf, I wish you, above all, enjoyment in what you do.

Peter Smith
1993

The Professionals

Peter Dawson turned professional in 1971, having enjoyed a sparkling amateur career, representing his country at almost every level. In 1977 he was a member of the European Ryder Cup team, and partnered Nick Faldo in the World Cup later that year, representing England.

After a career at golf clubs in Britain, he was appointed Head Professional at Hardelot, France, in 1989 and was the Danish National Coach for three years.

He is now the National Coach to the Swiss Golf teams. He is also on the panel of elite coaches for Golf World Teaching Schools, and writes regular instruction columns for Golf World magazine.

Stuart Little trained in golf course design and management before taking up the game as a professional in 1984, when he became assistant at Minchinhampton, near Stroud.

From 1985 to 1987 he played almost full time, in PGA events in Britain.

In 1991 he qualified from the Tour School to play on the European Tour, finishing a commendable 9th at the Monte Carlo Open in his first season. He also ended the 1992 season as the second longest driver overall, with an average drive of 185 yards. He qualified again for the 1993 European Tour season.

Apart from his European Tour commitments Stuart remains attached to Minchinhampton Golf Club.

Simon Mayfield is the Professional at Haverhill Golf Club in Suffolk, where his teaching skills, particularly with junior county teams, has made him a highly respected and much sought-after coach. Prior to moving to Haverhill in 1986, Simon served a demanding apprenticeship as assistant professional at Southwood GC, Farnborough, the Army Golf Club and at both Kettering and Kendall.

At Kettering he teamed up with, and served under Peter Thomson, whose expertise in understanding and teaching the technique of the swing is recognised as second to none. Simon is also an expert club maker and repairer.

Nick Brace has been playing golf since he was 12 years old though, unlike many young golfers, decided that he wanted to become a club professional rather than being attracted by the glamour of the European Tour.

Turning professional in 1981 he served four years as assistant professional at Warren GC, Wallasey. From 1985 to 1988 he was Senior Assistant at Wirral Ladies GC, where his teaching technique was hugely successful.

He became Professional at West Derby GC, Liverpool in 1988.

In 1984 and 1985 he reached the final of the National Assistants' Championship.

Although this is not a complete list the following are some of the most respected left handed golf professionals in Britain:

Nick Brace
W Derby G.C., Liverpool

Simon Mayfield
Haverhill G.C., Haverhill, Suffolk

Stuart Little
Minchinhampton G.C., Stroud, Gloucestershire

Robin Lawrie
Seacroft G.C., Skegness, Lincolnshire

Jason Mitchell
Thorpe Wood G.C., Peterborough, Cambridgeshire

Martin Evans
Normanton G.C., Normanton, Yorkshire

Richard Tinworth
West Malling G.C., Addington, Maidstone, Kent

Peter Dawson is based in northern France, just 20 minutes drive from the Boulogne ferry terminal.

Peter Dawson
Golfs d'Hardelot, France

Getting started

grip, stance, alignment and the golf swing

Alignment

Good golfers always approach the ball from behind, clearly "seeing" the line to the target.

Many people who take up golf believe that getting the grip right is the first thing they have to master. I have to say that, whilst the grip is vitally important to becoming a competent golfer, I always try to get the beginner to understand how to target the club before anything else. As good golf depends on hitting a small ball to a small target some hundreds of yards away it is not difficult to understand why targeting is so important.

After all, in any sport where you use a ball you will only succeed if you can get that ball on target. To get it on target you have to aim correctly in the first place.

Our first priority, then, is to aim correctly. This is so for golfers of any ability, from the absolute beginner to the Open champion. Indeed, players like Nick Faldo or Fred Couples aim the club **before** they take their grip, every single time. Watch them as they set up for a shot. First they stand behind the ball and pick an imaginary line from the ball to the target. Then they put the club head on the ground behind the ball to aim the club. Then, when they are happy with that, they take their grip. You should do the same, every time. Make it a habit.

Hold the club, in one hand if you choose, with the club head on the ground about a half inch behind the ball and with the centre of the club face level with the centre of the ball.

Ensure that the leading edge (the bottom groove on the club face) is exactly at right angles to the target.

When you are starting at golf, or at any time when you want to recheck your set up, something you should do often, lay a club on the ground from the ball along the target line and check your aim.

This is something you can do at home, indoors if you wish, as you do not need to swing or hit the ball to get it right.

The next stage is to align your body parallel to the target line. This, once again, you should recheck regularly; again you can do it at home.

Lay another club on the ground parallel to the first one going from the

Your feet should be parallel to the ball-to-target line.

ball towards the target. This second club will give you the correct alignment for your feet. Then check that your knees and shoulders are all perfectly aligned.

More bad shots are hit in golf due to poor alignment and targeting than anything else, so check and recheck regularly.

You can now check the position of the ball in your stance.

The ball should be very slightly forward of centre of your stance. Again you can check this with a third club on the

Align the club face first, using the very bottom groove of the club as your guide.

Your shoulders also need to be parallel to the ball-to-target line. That should help square up your knees as well.

ground, before you get ready to hit every single shot in your round of golf. Just by lining up properly you will probably save at least half a dozen shots each round, no matter what your ability. If top professionals of the calibre of Ballesteros, Couples, Norman and others all take a couple of seconds to check their alignment before each shot then you can be sure it will benefit you. Get into the habit of doing it every time.

If you wish to contact the ball perfectly you must have the ball in the perfect position in your stance.

ground as shown in the photograph. When you take your final address position the hands need to be just ahead of the ball, not directly above it. This, when you come to hit the ball, will help ensure that you hit down into the back of the ball rather than trying to scoop it up.

Although it may seem time-consuming you really should adopt this procedure, without laying additional clubs on the

The set up is vitally important and you really must regularly check that you are in the right position.

Left: The club head has been aligned correctly and the feet are parallel to the ball-to-target line, but the shoulders are not correctly aligned. This could easily cause a slice.

Right: Once the alignment is correct the ball position and grip need checking. On the practice ground you have the chance to do this using extra clubs laid on the ground. It helps to train your eyes.

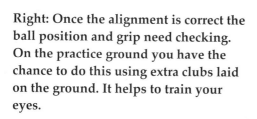

Your Grip

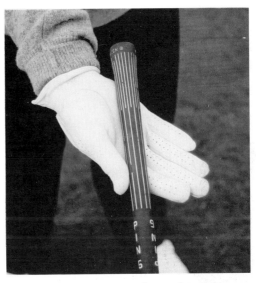

Now you are ready to take your grip, the right hand first. Let your right hand just hang loose by your side. You will notice the natural curling of the fingers. Keeping the club head on the ground in its square position, take hold of the club with your right hand, the right thumb pointing straight down the centre of the shaft. The fingers then wrap themselves around the grip, but you need to understand where the club grip lays in the right hand.

The "heel" of the hand is opposite the pad at the base of the thumb and the end of the club should lay across this, with about half an inch overlapping. The club then lays diagonally across the centre of the hand and across the first joint of the index finger.

The fingers then wrap round the club so that the two middle fingers just touch the pad at the base of the thumb. If they don't touch you should either grip further down the shaft a little (it narrows from the top downwards) or get smaller grips fitted to your clubs. If either of those two fingers overlap the thumb pad you might need larger grips, or you have not taken the grip correctly. Ask your club professional for advice as getting the grip right

Above: The club lays across the right hand from the heel of the hand to the first joint on the index finger.
Below: The two middle fingers should just touch the thumb pad.

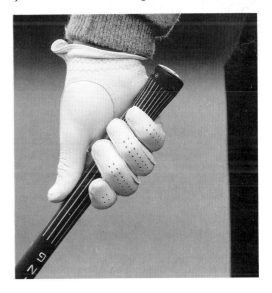

often requires only a tiny adjustment.

The back of your right hand should be pointing directly towards the target, as shown by the club laying across your feet. You should also be able to see just two knuckles on your right hand, but as it can be difficult to do this when looking down, I suggest you hold the club up in the air, as the photograph below shows. This will give you a better indication as to whether your hand is in the correct position. You may need to very slightly adjust it until you are in the correct position, but do remember to keep the club head square; you turn your grip, not the club!

When you hold the club upright you should see two knuckles on your right hand.

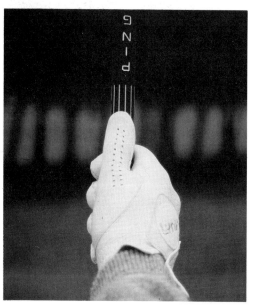

Now for the left hand and there are a couple of variations. Most people, and the vast majority of professionals, use the Vardon grip, named after the Jersey professional who won the British Open a record six times in the early twentieth century. It is the best grip possible as it keeps the two hands firmly in place throughout the stroke, leading to better accuracy and a firmer shot.

The little finger of the left hand should overlap the groove between the first two fingers of the right hand, the remaining fingers wrapping around the club.

Harry Vardon won the British Open a record six times. His grip has never been improved upon.

Although the club is held more in the palm of the right hand, in the left hand it is the fingers which hold the club.

There is a slight gap between the index and middle fingers as the index finger is slightly triggered for more control. The left thumb holds the shaft very slightly to the right of centre; the index finger grips it more to the left of centre. Don't let too large a gap appear between your index finger and thumb of that left hand or you will lose control as you swing.

The thumb pad of the left hand covers the right thumb, making a snug but not overly tight fit.

The "V"s formed by your thumb and index finger joints should both be pointing at the same place, a point midway between your chin and left shoulder.

You may now need to make a very slight adjustment, fine tuning the grip. The "V"s formed by the joint of the thumbs and index fingers should be pointing in the same direction, ideally a point midway between your chin and right shoulder. Without turning the club, which should still be square to the target, loosen your hands and rotate them very slightly until they are in this position, then again tighten your hold on the club.

The left thumb pad covers the right thumb, making a snug fit.

You now have the correct grip. As I said there are a couple of variations to the Vardon grip, but they do all look the same from the front and they all keep the club square throughout the swing.

Some golfers with small hands may find the interlocking grip easier to use. Several professionals, including Jack Nicklaus, have used this variation. It is the same as the Vardon with one tiny change: the little finger of the left hand, instead of laying over the top of the right index finger, interlocks with it - hence the name.

Golfers with small hands may find the ten finger grip more comfortable, though the hands must be kept tightly together.

Jack Nicklaus achieved success with an interlocking grip. Ben Hogan used a very similar grip.

The other variation is often used by players with small hands, including many women and younger golfers. It involves having all ten fingers on the club, though they still maintain a snug fit.

Whatever grip you use the main thing is that the hands should work together as a single unit. Go back to your grip time and time again, checking and rechecking that it is correct. That is the only way to ensure that you have the right basics to play good golf on a consistent basis.

The Stance

We now move on to the stance. One question which everyone asks is: how wide should the stance be? The answer is that it should be wide enough to maintain your balance but not that wide that it restricts your turn. Too wide a stance can

Bend from the hips with your knees slightly bent. You should keep your spine as straight as possible, but always be athletically poised, not rigid.

Your feet need to be wide enough apart for you to maintain your balance, but not too wide or you risk swaying.

cause you to sway on the back swing rather than turn around the pivot. In practice, because everyone is of a different height and build, having your feet approximately shoulder width apart is the ideal.

With your feet aligned parallel to the club on the ground indicating the target line, you should turn your toes outwards very slightly. Again, this helps with the balance as you turn.

Your posture needs to be athletic, your weight equal all round - not too much on either side nor too much to the front or back. Your spine needs to be fairly straight though inclined forward from the hips. It is important to bend from the hips rather than the waist as this will help you to maintain the correct posture through the swing.

As you will see from the photograph on the previous page, the body bends on three distinct, straight lines.

At address the hands are held slightly ahead of the ball, helping to promote a consistently good position at impact, the club descending onto the ball.

Leave enough room between your hands and thighs to enable your arms to swing the club through freely.

Though simplified, this is something you should keep in mind if you want to swing properly.

There needs to be sufficient room between the hands (holding the club) and the legs for the arms to swing freely and the body to turn. You can judge the correct distance by taking one hand off the club and, with the palm open, hold the hand between the club shaft and the right thigh. Your hand should fit in the gap, depending on the size of your hands, of course. The main thing to remember is that you should feel comfortable yet athletically poised.

So far we have set up with the weight evenly distributed. Do not forget what we said earlier though, about having the hands slightly ahead of the ball, rather than directly above them. A line drawn from the club head up the shaft and up the right arm to the shoulder should be more or less straight, though not stiff.

Because the left hand is lower on the club than the right, it is pretty obvious that the left shoulder will be a little lower as you address the ball, but beware of turning the shoulders to an open position (a line across the shoulders pointing right of the ball to target line).

Much of this set up is difficult to check for yourself so either get a friend to check these points carefully for you or take up your address position at home in front of a full length mirror. Only by repeating the set up procedure over and over again will you be able to get it right on a consistent basis.

The final point, before we get on to actually swinging the club, is to make sure you keep your head up away from your chest. Don't drop your chin too much or you will not be able to turn properly. Your head should stay fairly still throughout the swing. You should aim to keep it as still as you can, though it is impossible to keep perfectly still.

We have now completed the set-up procedure, which may sound rather long-winded at this stage but once you begin doing it regularly it will take only a few seconds. Get into the habit of rechecking your grip, alignment and posture before every shot if you want to play to the best of your ability.

Always keep your head well up away from your chest at address or you will knock your chin as you swing your shoulders, knocking your head out of its position above the body pivot.

The Swing

O nce the grip and set up are mastered the next thing to do is actually swing the club to hit the ball.

To achieve a good swing you have to turn the body round its pivot, creating a spring-like force which, when released, powers the swing.

The back swing is begun by the rotation of the shoulders, but the right arm remains straight at this stage.

Note how the body turns round its pivot on the back swing, rather than swaying.

The pivot is an imaginary line from the top of the spine down the back to a point directly above the centre of the stance.

The first movement in the back swing is to turn the left shoulder backwards, at the same time keeping the arms and club extended. As the shoulders turn the club comes back inside the ball to target line, but at this stage you should aim to keep the wrists fairly firm, avoiding what is known as "picking the club up" on the back swing. This term refers to the incorrect action of bending, or cocking, the wrists too early in the back swing.

As the shoulders turn and the club swings up and back the hips will also begin turning to the left. The right knee will kick in and left slightly; the right heel may be raised very slightly off the ground as the weight transfers to the left side. Try not to raise the right heel too much as it can cause you to momentarily lose your balance.

Balance can also be lost if you sway on the back swing, your hips moving to the left laterally rather than turning.

To help wind up the power you need to keep your left knee flexed, thus creating the tension needed.

At the top of the back swing the club goes to about horizontal. Note how straight the right arm is to increase the width of the arc and produce extra club head speed at impact.

The left leg, though very slightly bent, should take the strain on the back swing, restricting the hips from turning any more than about 45°. The shoulders, though, continue and complete a 90° turn. The left leg must remain firm, the hips turning above it rather than the leg moving to one side.

At the top of the back swing the club should be pointing almost directly along the target line, close to horizontal. The right arm should, at this point, be as straight as you can keep it, though not locked. This is one of the secrets of power in the swing, though you should not try to get the club too far over until you are more competent at golf. Build up to it gradually.

Then comes the down swing, which is not really a separate movement but part of one flowing movement which reverses as you reach the top of the back swing.

To kick start the down swing push your right foot flat, beginning the transfer of weight to your right side. As you do this move your hips laterally towards the right, ahead of the ball. At the same time your hips are turning clockwise, pulling your shoulders round. That, in turn, pulls your arms, and the club head, down towards impact.

At impact the hips and hands are just ahead of the ball, promoting a firm downward strike into the ball. Note how the head has maintained its address position, very slightly behind the ball.

The down swing begins with the hips moving laterally and the arms pulling down.

Note how, in the follow through, the left knee has kicked round to face the target as the arms continue to swing the club to a full finish.

As the arms swing down try to keep the right arm still fairly straight; don't let it bend too much or you will lose power in the swing and probably slice the ball left.

By the time you reach the impact position your hips should be aiming off very slightly to the right, your shoulders square to the target; this provides enough room for the arms to swing through to a correct finish. If you have not turned enough your arms get tangled up with your hips and you can not strike the ball properly.

Your arms should be straight as you accelerate the club head into the ball, thus creating extra power. I would stress again, though, that the hips must be ahead of the ball at impact.

The follow through is often neglected yet is very important. Too many golfers fail to maintain acceleration through the ball; this will cause them to hit the ball poorly, without harnessing the power they have created in the back swing. After impact keep turning the body to the right so that, as you finish, the entire body is facing the target. The left foot, you will notice, has turned and is on tip toe to help get the body round into position.

This, then, is the swing technique. It may sound complicated but is not, as long as you remember that it is one smoothly flowing movement rather than many different ones.

The next couple of pages show it in slow motion, with each main part clearly described.

The Swing in sequence:

Above Left: From a well aligned address position the arms swing the club back as the shoulders begin to rotate.

Below Left: At the top of the back swing the shoulders have made a full turn, the hips have half turned; the head is fairly still above the pivot and the right arm is fairly straight, lengthening the arc.

Above Right: As you begin the down swing the hips move laterally and begin to turn, the arms pull down hard but the wrists remain cocked for as long as possible.

Above Left: At impact the wrists have released to bring the club face square to the ball, the hips have cleared but the head remains just behind the ball.

Above Right: Just after impact the arms have straightened as the club is swung through the ball rather than at it. The body is continuing to turn to face the target and the head is just beginning to move.

Below Right: At the finish the body has completed its turn, the left knee having turned fully and the arms having swung the club right through. A perfect finish position.

The Short Game

The Short Game

The short game is one of the most important parts of golf. There are many occasions when you don't quite make it onto the green, particularly with your second shot on a long par-4, leaving you with a testing little chip or pitch to get close enough to save par.

There are other holes which, being less lengthy, leave the golfer with a shot into the green of around 100 yards or so; this is often the case on a par-5 hole where two good shots will leave a tantalising shot of maybe 80 yards or so. Getting the ball close to the pin in those circumstances can not only mean a safe par but a possible birdie.

It is fairly obvious, then, that a good short game, like putting, can quickly lower both your score and your handicap, and do wonders for your confidence. It is also a part of the game which everyone can improve, because it does not take enormous power, but rather finesse and technique.

We start our look at the short game at its shortest, just off the green. This is the place to learn the technique. We shall then move back down the fairway to about 100 yards and you will see that virtually nothing changes in the set up or technique. The only alteration we make is in the length of the back swing.

You might not have thought it was that simple but I can assure you it is. There is no magic formula or secret known only to professionals, just plain common sense and a sound basic technique that every golfer can use.

On occasions like this, with about 80 yards to the pin, an accurate approach shot could make all the difference to your final score.

Our first situation is one of those little chips from just off the green where we have about two yards of semi-rough to carry before we reach the safety of the green itself. The pin, on this occasion, is on the other side of the green and we are thus faced with, in effect, a long putt, the first couple of yards of which just happens to be over some semi rough rather than the lush surface of the green.

Your first choice is: what type of shot and what club? When you approach the ball you will have first thoughts about the shot. You might see it as a long putt; you

A shot from semi-rough round the green becomes, in effect, a long putt. Treat it that way.

might see it as a chip and run; or you might see it as a pitch almost directly at the pin. Much will depend on your confidence in your ability to play these three types of shot, but you will also be taking into account the condition of the semi-rough and the lie of the ball, any slope on the green, and the speed of the green itself. In winter and wet weather the greens are usually a little slower. In mid summer with a hot sun beating down they can be very fast.

If the greens are medium speed, the lie is good and there are no muddy patches, worm casts or anything else between the ball and the edge of the green, your best shot is probably a long putt.

I shall leave putting technique out here as it is dealt with elsewhere, but I must emphasise the point that, whichever shot you see in your mind when you reach the ball, stick with it unless there are very clear circumstances which make you change your mind.

You must be positive about the shot and having second thoughts halfway through the swing will only result in a poor shot.

You should remember that, for most golfers, a poor putt is better than a poor chip; and a poor chip is better than a poor pitch. The putt is the easiest option and so, if conditions permit and that is the shot you are happiest with, then putt it.

The second option, one you might choose if the ground is a little muddy, the

Once you have made your choice of shot be positive and don't change your mind.

over the long grass and onto the putting surface. Once it lands it just runs like a normal putt.

You need to "see" the ball landing on the green and running smoothly at the hole. Incidentally, you can leave the flag in if you are off the green; should you hit it there is no penalty.

Decide where the ball should land to begin its roll and then align the club face, just as you do with every other shot, with the bottom groove exactly square to the target.

grass round the ball long or just too much long grass between the ball and the safety of the green to make a putt sensible, is a chip and run. This is one of the easiest shots in golf, yet one which surprisingly high numbers of golfers get wrong.

You may have heard a lot about visualising a shot, which we shall deal with it later in this book. On a shot like this it is important to "see" the shot in its entirety before playing it.

A chip and run is really just like a long putt, but with the ball getting airborne for the first couple of yards in order to get it

Alignment is just as important on a short shot as it is on any other. The ball goes where you aim it.

For this exercise we are imagining that the green is flat, so the target is the flag, but bear in mind that if you have a sloping green you will need to judge the amount of borrow, so your target might not be the flag.

Your feet should be fairly close together to avoid swaying, but do maintain your balance.

I should perhaps, just explain the term "borrow" which you will often hear used in golf. When a putting green is not flat and you have to putt across the slope, you need to aim the ball to one side of the hole to allow it to follow the contours of the slope and finish near the hole. You have to "borrow" some of the slope, hence the term.

Having aligned the club face you next align your body. A short shot is really just an arms and shoulders movement with virtually no leg action. Remember what we have said about a chip and run being just like a long putt. When putting you hardly move your legs. It's the same on this chip and run.

Yet the arms need to swing through freely. On a full swing you turn your body through on the down swing to make room for the arms to swing the club through. Because there is little lower body movement on this shot you need to create enough room for the arms to swing through. You do this by very slightly opening your stance, your feet and shoulders pointing off a little to the right of the target.

Stand with your feet reasonably close together, but maintain your balance. Having too wide a stance could make you sway, something you definitely do not want on this shot.

The ball should be fairly well forward in your stance and importantly, your hands are well ahead of the ball. This

Note the almost straight line from club head to shoulder, with the hands ahead of the ball.

automatically puts about 65% of your weight on your right foot.

As you can see from the photograph above there is virtually a straight line from the club head up through the shaft and right arm to the shoulder. This is the perfect address position for this shot.

It is the perfect address position because it is the perfect *impact* position. Remember that the golf swing is intended to get the club head back to the ball at impact in exactly the same position you had at address. Remember that and your golf will improve.

Your grip will be as normal, but you might find it helpful to grip further down the club for extra control.

By the way for this shot I recommend a 7-iron, rather than a wedge. It varies according to the distance the ball needs to roll once it lands. A more lofted club will get the ball higher with less roll once it lands. For this shot the pin is fifteen yards away across the green, so we want to fly it maybe five yards and let it roll the rest of the way.

A number of golfers make a mess of this shot because they swing the club back too far; then, fearing that they will over-hit the ball, they slow the club down as it approaches the ball, resulting in more of a stab that gets the ball nowhere.

The secret is in the relative lengths of the back swing and the through swing. The former must be much shorter than the latter. Imagine for a moment that you are standing in the same position, just off the green and need to throw a golf ball underarm, to land near the flag. Try it. You will immediately notice that on the back swing, your arm only moves back a short distance. Yet the follow through is much longer, with your arm and hand finishing pointing at the target and virtually horizontal. You do the same with the golf club.

A short back swing is enough to allow you to accelerate the club head forward through impact to the finish. The club head finishes in the same position as your hand did when you threw the ball.

As with a putt your wrists stay firm throughout the swing, with no cocking on the back swing or release as you come through impact. In fact if you look carefully you will notice that the wrists are already hinged at address, as they are pressing the club forward ahead of the ball. They stay in that position throughout the swing. Don't try to flick at the ball either, just keep the hands in position and accelerate the club head through impact.

A major fault of many golfers is to swing back too far and then to decelerate the club into impact when they suddenly realise they are going to over hit it.

Remember to swing back 40% and through 60%.

Above: When you throw a ball under-arm your arm comes back only a short distance . . .
Right: . . . but follows through further.

Let's now move back a little further to a shot which often causes problems to even experienced golfers. We are now forty yards from the flag and have a bunker between the ball and the green. It is, in this case, a fairly flat bunker rather than one which towers in front of us. All we need to do is to get the ball over the bunker and onto the green where, once again, it will roll to the hole.

Many players would automatically reach for the wedge here but I am again going to suggest the trusty 7-iron. Why?

If there was no bunker we would quite happily chip the ball ten yards onto the front of the green and let it run. As the bunker is not high, nor very long, we still only have to chip the ball ten yards and let it run. It is the same shot we have just played, except a little longer. That means that the set up is exactly the same but the back swing, and thus through swing, are a little longer. Nothing else changes. Even if the bunker was high and we needed a wedge to get the ball airborne quickly, virtually nothing in the technique changes. But back to the shot over the low bunker.

Why do many golfers fear this shot?

For this shot you could stand slightly open to the target, which helps to restrict your back swing.

The club face still points at the target at address, the hands are still well forward of the ball, keeping a straight line from the ball to the right shoulder. The feet and shoulders may be a little less open, and the feet may be slightly wider apart. You will notice that, as you stand open to the target your back swing is restricted, which is what we want on this shot.

A hazard, like a bunker or a lake, always adds an extra psychological problem to most golfers, and as a consequence

the majority of players would feel they have to hit a wedge in these circumstances. That is not the case, however. This is the same type of shot as the last one, so only needs a 7-iron to get the ball airborne for a few yards before landing on the front of the green and rolling to the hole.

A major fault of many golfers is when they try to get extra height on the ball by increasing the loft of the club. You can, of course, if you need more height, use a more lofted club. You can also increase the loft on the club you are using by opening your stance more. What many golfers do is to turn the club face more open and this is where their problems begin.

The ball will go in the direction the club face is pointing, so if it is open the ball will go off to the left too far.

You must keep the club face square to the target. To get more loft on the club you adjust *your* position and alignment, not the club face. Turn your feet more to the right but don't alter the club face.

The back swing needs to be a little longer this time but again keep in mind the 40/60 ratio between back swing and through swing. Once again, there is very little lower body movement, though as the length of the swing increases your shoulders will turn more and your legs will automatically begin to move more.

Do guard against swaying, either on the back swing or on the way through. As we shall see in a moment that can cause you to flick at the ball, often topping it. You can see the result of this shot clearly in the photograph on page 39, the straight line from club head to shoulder being broken. At address that line is straight, at impact it is straight and it should be straight at the finish. If it is not you have used too much wrist movement and you won't get the best results from your shot.

With all chip and run shots the important thing is to visualise where you want

Don't forget the 40/60 ratio for all short shots. Below is the back swing . . .

. . . and above the follow through.

the ball to land, not where you want it to finish.

Moving back even further we reach a position some eighty yards from the pin, with a bunker still to carry before we reach the safety of the green. This is where we need height on the ball as we want to carry it virtually the whole way to the pin before stopping it quickly.

You will have seen professionals at tournaments hitting these shots high into the heart of the green before bringing the ball spinning back to within inches of the hole. Hitting a ball with that amount of backspin is difficult for the average golfer, particularly if you are not using the balata golf balls favoured by the professionals. However well you hit it, a normal surlyn covered golf ball will not spin back much, but as most club golfers leave the ball short of the pin you probably don't want to.

For this fuller shot, using here a wedge or 9-iron, whichever you feel most comfortable with for the distance and your ability, your stance is virtually square to

On the longer shot to the green the back swing just increases in length; everything else remains virtually the same.

The follow through is also much longer, more like the finish of any other shot.

the target and your hands are not pressed forward so much.

On the back swing your wrists will automatically cock as the club swings back up to maybe three-quarters. Your shoulders will turn as on a normal swing and on the way back through impact your hips will clear to the right, giving the arms and club room to swing through.

Once again you must continue to accelerate through impact; you adjust the length of the shot by the length of your back swing. Once again you should keep in mind that 40/60 ratio.

We mentioned earlier that many golfers try to flick at the ball in an attempt to get extra height on it. This can lead to you leaning backwards through impact and into the follow through, as the photograph opposite clearly shows.

As we found in the first section of this book, when dealing with the swing itself, your hips are moving ahead of the ball at impact so you are always hitting down into the ball rather than trying to scoop it up.

If you work the wrists too much you will break the shoulder/club line and end up flicking at the shot.

Don't lean back as you follow through. Never try to scoop the ball up.

You will see that all of these shots, from the little chip just off the green, back to the chip over the bunker to the full wedge shot, the basics of the swing have stayed the same. All that varies is the length of the back swing. A longer back swing moves the lower body more, so it appears that it is different but it is not. Get the short shots right and the longer shots become easier too.

The art to getting the ball the correct distance is to get the length of the back swing correct and then to keep accelerating through the ball. Never "quit" on the shot by slowing the club down as you approach impact out of fear that you are going to over hit it.

Before we leave the short game I think it is worth just going back briefly over the main points, particularly as the short game is so important. Even if you are not a long hitter your short game could help you save par almost every time.

Below: Get into the habit of looking from behind the ball down the target line, carefully choosing the line you need. Take note of any slopes the ball may have to roll across on its way to the hole, just as you would when putting.

Above: Get your address position right. Your hands are ahead of the ball, with a virtually straight line from the right shoulder to the club head, your feet are not too far apart and you are athletically poised but never stiff. The swing is one smoothly flowing movement.

Setting the hands just ahead of the ball helps to cock the wrists early which is what you want, though don't overdo it.

Above: You must move the club back smoothly; never be tempted to pick it up too steeply as that will ruin the shot. You must also let it swing inside the line naturally rather than holding it straight. At this stage your head has remained over the pivot, eyes firmly on the ball.

Below: As the back swing progresses you can see the wrists have cocked more to get length in the swing. Despite this there is not too much leg movement and the shoulders are not completing their turn.

Below: The down swing is begun by the right foot pushing flat and the hips turning to the right and moving laterally so that they are out of the way as the arms swing the club down. Note how still the head has stayed at this point.

Above: At the top of the back swing the head is still beautifully poised above the pivot and you can see that the three-quarter swing has resulted in the shoulders not turning fully; the hips have also only turned a little.

The wrist cock has given the club head its extra distance and can now be accelerated down into the back of the ball. Never rush the swing on a short shot. You should "feel" it.

Below: Just after impact the head is still "down", as the hips have continued rotating to clear the way for the club to strike the ball and, importantly, to swing through it. The club head is still continuing, having just passed its maximum speed as it hit the ball.

Above: And finally the finishing position. The body has turned to face the target giving the arms room to swing the club through, slowing down as it climbs. You must never try to stop the club; let it slow down of its own accord. The left knee has kicked round but the poise and balance are still there.

Bunkers

Bunkers

Most golfers, with the exception of professionals, have a fear of bunkers which, before they even begin thinking about getting the ball out, is adding to the pressure they are imposing on themselves.

This fear is based more on their lack of understanding about what they should be doing rather than an inability to do it. Watching any professional at a tournament on television will prove to you that, with the correct technique, the ball will come out first time, every time, and often land fairly close to the pin.

The extra strength and length of shot professionals undoubtedly have doesn't matter here, as it is not a long shot, but one which entails touch and finesse. It does, though, demand a full swing and this is what lets most golfers down.

There are, of course, occasions when the ball is in a difficult position, particularly if it is plugged or on a downslope at the back of the bunker, and in such a circumstance getting it near the pin may be a little over-ambitious. Sometimes your best shot will be the safest and that might mean splashing the ball out to a different part of the green and having a

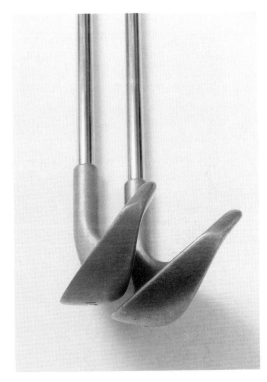

The sand wedge, unlike other clubs, has a wide flange which bounces off the sand rather than digging in.

long putt or two. That, is, however, much better than leaving the ball in the sand.

We are going to look at several bunker situations but I want to begin with the basic bunker shot where the ball is sitting nicely on top of the sand, the bunker face is not too steep, there is plenty of green to work with and the sand is dry.

The sand wedge is made with a wide

flange which, instead of digging into the sand, as any other club would do, literally bounces through the sand. What it does is to get under the ball and lift out a cushion of sand. It is that cushion of sand which lifts the ball out, not the club. The secret of good bunker play is not to hit the ball, but to hit the sand.

To play a normal, straightforward bunker shot stand with the ball opposite your right heel as you stand square to the target, in this case the flag. There is much confusion over the ball position and the club face position in bunker shots. On a normal shot from the fairway you set up with your feet and body square to the target, the club face also square and the ball aligned with your right heel.

Do the same here to begin with, aligning the club face very carefully, for where the club face points is where the ball will go. Be careful not to ground the club in the sand as that is a penalty stroke, though if you are in the practice bunker at your local club you could do it to ensure you get that club face alignment correct.

Without turning the club face move your feet into a slightly open position, bringing your right foot back a little from the target line. Your shoulders and hips

Below Left: The ball is positioned just off the right heel to begin with . . .

Below Right: . . . but then you turn your feet to an open position so the ball appears to be further back in your stance.

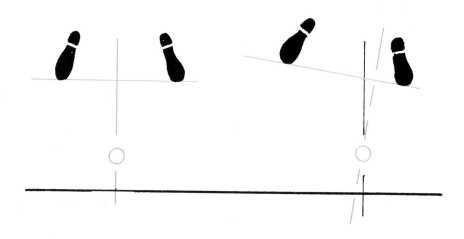

follow this line so that a club held across your chest would now point right of the target. It is vital, though, that you do not change the alignment of the club face. That must still be pointing at the flag.

You are now standing open to the target and the ball will appear to be further back in your stance, though in truth it is not.

Your weight should probably be about 60% on your right side, so that you are leaning slightly towards the green. In this position your hands are ahead of the ball.

Your weight should be about 60% on your right foot.

This position helps you to hit down behind the ball, which is what you want. Ideally you should be aiming to hit the club into the sand about an inch or so behind the ball.

Now for the swing and it is this which defeats a large number of golfers. Because the ball is so close to the green it is a fairly natural thought process to believe that the shot does not need to be made with a full swing, but rather a little stab at the ball. After all, if you were chipping the ball this distance you would only swing your arms back and through a very short distance.

You must always align the club face to the target. Do it before you take your grip.

This assumption is totally wrong. A bunker shot must be played with a fairly full (at least a three-quarter) swing, both back and through. Your first reaction to this is that you will probably hit the ball miles, but the only time the ball will fly way over the green is if you *thin* it, catching the ball rather than the sand. It is the speed of the hands that count, as you will see when we reach the lesson on driving for power. A full, slow swing with a gentle rhythm hitting the sand just behind the ball is what you need.

Try it. Go to your golf course, get into the practice bunker and, providing the sand is dry and fairly powdery, rather than gritty or wet, you can hit as hard as you like and the ball will splash out fairly gently. You must hit the sand, though, not the ball.

Other mistaken theories about bunker play are that you have to "pick the club up" steeply on the back swing, and that you have to break the wrists early. Both are wrong. The wrists are already broken, or cocked, just by the way you are standing with your hands slightly ahead of the ball and your weight favouring your right side.

You must take a fairly full back swing if you are to get the ball out first time. The view from face on and down the line.

Swing the club back smoothly and slowly; never pick it up too steeply.

Also, it is not really necessary on most straightforward bunker shots to pick the club up steeply. Just swing normally, up to about three-quarters length. The secret, if there is one, is to swing slowly, and this takes courage.

I have mentioned the fear of hitting the ball too far out of a bunker. What you must remember is that if your back swing is too fast, the downswing will be too fast. Then, halfway through the downswing your brain will suddenly realise you are going too fast and the natural reaction is to slow down. The arms and hands thus begin to slow the swing down, with the almost inevitable result that you are slowing the club down at exactly that moment when it needs most speed, as it hits into the sand and through impact.

This is often referred to as "quitting" on the shot and will more often than not result in the ball staying in the sand. You need to try this to fully believe it and I hope you will do so. You must swing slowly, though, almost painfully so, particularly in the back swing. Then, as the arms begin to pull the club down gravity lends a hand and the club head picks up speed. It needs to be at its maximum speed as it enters the sand just behind the

You need a full follow through; never quit on a bunker shot.

ball. Then, continuing upwards to a full, high finish, the club slows as it reaches the top of the follow-through.

It is important to follow through if you are to float the ball out. Don't try to stab at it.

When you are taking your stance you might find it helpful to shuffle your feet into the sand a little more, giving you a firmer footing. Because your hands are ahead of the ball and your weight favouring the right foot, the wrists will cock quickly and naturally.

The bunker shot is more of an arms and shoulders swing with little lower body or leg movement.

As you swing try to keep the feet securely planted, so the swing is more of an upper body, arms and shoulders swing rather than using the lower body. The bunker shot swing really is a hands and arms movement, effortless and slow, but full. We want the hands to control the shot with very little lower body or leg movement.

Plugged lies

Not all bunker shots are, of course, straightforward and there are many occasions when you are faced with a far more difficult shot. Some of these shots may, as I said earlier, have to be away from the flag. Always keep in mind that your first priority is to get the ball out of the sand and safely onto the putting surface if at all possible.

Better to have a long putt than another bunker shot!

I am going to look first at "plugged" lies, where the ball is almost buried, often in fairly soft sand. Once again you must remember that you need a fairly full swing, at least three-quarter length so that, at the top of the back swing, your hands have reached at least shoulder height.

Because the ball is plugged it becomes impossible to get any backspin on it, thus making it difficult to control. If you only have a small amount of green to work with you might find it safer to play to a wider part of the green rather than going directly at the flag.

A plugged lie demands that you stand almost square to the target, rather than

The bunker shot every golfer hates - a plugged ball.

open. You can be very slightly open, but not too much. You must have the club face square to the target though - the ball will always go where you aim it. Grip down the club a little more for greater control if you find this more comfortable.

Your weight will be around 60% to your front foot, again putting your hands very slightly ahead of the ball. In this position your wrists are already slightly cocked, so don't worry about trying to do that as it happens naturally. You should also have the ball a little further back in your stance than normal, as the aim is to hit down into the back of the ball this time, rather than sliding the sand wedge under the ball.

By adopting this squarer set up you are, in effect, stopping the sand wedge from doing its job. If you recall, the sand wedge is made with a wide flange which slides underneath the ball, bouncing off the sand and lifting the ball out on a cushion of sand. With it plugged the flange of the sand wedge would hit into the sand and bounce before it has managed to get under the ball. The result is that it would hit the ball itself, digging it further into the sand or would decelerate so much that it would not have the power to get the ball out.

Our aim with a plugged lie is to hit down into the back of the ball, letting the lofted club face get the ball airborne very quickly without letting the sand wedge bounce. Unfortunately, because sand will get between the club face and the ball it is impossible to get a clean contact or the control that would give.

Depending on the consistency of the sand (the firmer it is the firmer you must hit the shot) you need a three-quarter swing, but still fairly slow, with the club

head accelerating as it approaches the ball. Because you are coming in at a steep angle the club face will dig into the sand and you will not be able to complete a full follow-through. You must not try to stop the club though as the sand will do that for you. As the club face hits the ball it needs to be going at its maximum speed for this swing.

If you have the courage, try swinging slowly on this shot too, though do ensure

A plugged lie demands a square stance and club face.

you are not decelerating the club head as you approach impact.

The result of this steep descent of the club into the ball is that you, in effect, stab at it, but you must not have that picture in your mind or you will end up slowing the club down, probably with the risk that the ball will remain in the sand. Hit hard.

For more advanced golfers, or if you have a good amount of green to work with, you might wish to use a pitching wedge here. The fact that it has no flange (like a sand wedge) means that its leading edge will dig straight into the sand rather than trying to bounce.

Putting from sand

In winter or when it has been raining heavily the sand in bunkers tends to get rather compacted. In certain circumstances I would suggest that you use a putter out of the sand, a suggestion that may surprise you.

Obviously, if you are in a high faced bunker that option is a non-starter, but if the bunker is reasonably flat with no overhanging lip and the sand is hard, the putter might be your best chance of getting the ball close to the pin.

Putting from sand takes courage but if you address the ball on the equator and hit it hard enough, provided the bunker has no steep face it will come out onto the green.

Line up just as you would for a long putt, being careful to note all the contours of the green and of the edge of the bunker; reading the line correctly is vital in this situation. Address the ball with the lower edge of the putter hovering above the sand, about level with the equator of the ball. You cannot touch the sand with the putter before you hit the ball, of course.

Depending on the length of shot, and remember the wet sand will hinder the ball and the wet green is likely to be slow as well, take a decent back swing and push the putter head through as you would on a long, uphill putt on the green. In the section on putting technique you will learn how important a follow through is on a putt. It is vital here, too.

This can be a very effective shot in the right circumstances and one you should practise when you have the chance. Although it will only arise rarely, when you do need to use it that experience of how to play it could mean the difference between saving par or dropping a couple of shots. Hitting a sand wedge out of wet sand is anything but easy and if you have another option, use it.

Sloping lies in bunkers

Of course not all bunkers are flat and we are often faced with either an up slope or a down slope in a bunker. Of the two the up slope is the easier shot so I shall deal with that first.

The main thing is to get yourself balanced, which may be easier said than done, as you might have to adopt a precarious position with one foot in the

bunker and the other outside. You might even have one leg bent almost double, or be on one knee, to make this shot, but however you have to stand, make sure you can swing your shoulders and arms without losing your balance.

On a shot like this your lower body hardly moves, the swing being made by the arms more than anything. Set up with your shoulders parallel to the slope, just as we did out on the fairway for an uphill lie. The weight is about 65% on your rear foot, hands ahead of the ball and your stance slightly open. Aim the club face directly at the flag and take a three-quarters swing, but as slowly as you can. Your follow-through might be cut off by the sand but do not attempt to decelerate the club. Hit through the ball as you should for a normal bunker shot, getting the sand wedge into the sand an inch or so behind the ball.

We then come to a more difficult shot where the ball is plugged on an upslope in the bunker, normally just below the ridge. Your prime concern here is to get the ball out over the ridge and onto the green and it is likely that you will have to hit the ball almost straight up in the air. Here, your weight should be on the front (right) foot but you may well have an awkward stance. You may well only have one foot in the bunker. Take your time getting your balance rather than rushing this shot.

The club face should be square to the

on this shot at all but you must feel that you are still accelerating as the club hits into the sand. If you quit on this, or any other bunker shot, you will leave the ball in the sand.

The majority of golfers either take an insufficient back swing, or fail to hit through the ball fully. Even when your follow through is restricted, do hit through. Remember to do these things and to swing smoothly and you will have no problems.

When the ball is plugged on an upslope in the bunker you set up with your shoulders leaning into the slope.

On an up slope in a bunker set up with your shoulders parallel to the slope.

target though, because of the way you are standing the club face is likely to be almost horizontal. Your weight is more to the right, so that you are leaning into the slope. You hit the club hard into the sand just below the ball. It should blast it out fairly high and you then hope that it will roll a little if you have some way to go to reach the pin. Because you hit it out high and almost vertically, to avoid catching the bunker ridge, it will land and stop quickly.

You will not be able to follow through

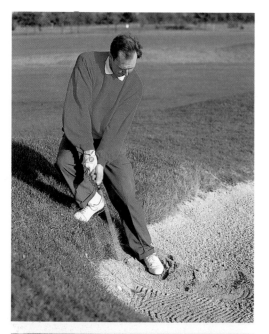

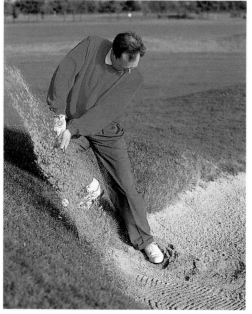

Downhill

The shots that are more difficult are those you often encounter at the back of the bunker, where you are faced with a down slope. Quite often the ball has just trickled into the bunker and could be quite close to the rear ridge of the bunker, making the take away difficult.

With this type of shot you are going to have a major problem stopping the ball on the green so you should be playing to the safest, that is largest, part of the green. As with almost all shots from sloping lies adjust your stance to the slope, so that your shoulders are parallel to the slope.

You need to stand with your feet line slightly open and you might find it more comfortable to grip down the club a little extra, for greater control. That open stance restricts your shoulder turn on the

Above Left: At address your main priority is to find a stance that will allow you to keep your balance. This can be rather difficult, but take your time.

Below Left: There will be very little follow through because the sand wedge just digs straight into the bunker, blasting the ball out.

On a downslope in a bunker you should set up with your weight on your forward foot, your shoulder line parallel to the slope.

Remember, set up level with the ground below your feet and then swing on that line. Don't fight nature. You will find more help in the section of this book where we deal with playing from sloping lies (see pages 63-70). A slope in a bunker is no different from anywhere else on the course.

Finally, before we leave greenside bunkers, remember that the swing needs to be at least three-quarter's length and as slow as you dare. A slow back swing inevitably means that the club will accelerate into the ball and that is what you want.

Mastering bunker shots will bring your

Never forget to take a fairly full swing in a bunker; never stab at the ball.

back swing, making you realise that this is, like all bunker shots, more of a hands, arms and shoulder movement than a lower body turn. The feet stay virtually still.

Because your shoulders are parallel to the slope your take away will appear steeper than if you were standing level, but this is an illusion and you should avoid the temptation to pick the club up on the back swing.

scores down significantly, quite often setting up the chance to save par rather than dropping a couple of shots.

Understanding that you need a full, slow swing that will accelerate the club head into the sand behind the ball will take away the fear of bunker shots that many golfers have. The place to try out this newly understood technique is the practice bunker at your local course. Perfect your technique there and you will

Always remember that a bunker shot, if it is to be successful, needs a full, slow swing - never stab at the ball, never quit on the shot.

approach bunker play with an entirely different attitude. With golf being such a "mind game" that immediately puts you in control of the situation.

Long Bunker Shots

Whilst we are dealing with bunkers we must not forget fairway bunkers. Many golf courses have these bunkers at or around the driving distance off the tee, normally in the 200-250 yard range; though there are many a little further forward, about 90 yards or so from the green, particularly on par-5s, designed to catch a good second shot. From the first position, with possibly a further 150-180 yards to the green the only sensible choice could be to knock the ball out of the bunker as far forward as is safe in the circumstances, leaving yourself with a short pitch to the green.

From a bunker 150 yards out the average golfer would find it difficult to land a ball safely on the green. In these circumstances the sensible suggestion has to be to play something like an 8-iron, moving the ball forwards into the fairway by about 100 yards or so.

There are other occasions when the ball is caught by a fairway bunker at about 120 yards from the green. In this case,

On a long bunker shot set up fairly square - your aim is to catch the ball cleanly.

providing the lie is good and the bunker not too deep or steep-faced, the aim could well be to land the ball on the green.

For either of these two situations I would suggest nothing longer than a 7-iron though you should always be looking to use one or two clubs more than you think you need for the distance. Thus if the distance suggests you should use a 9-iron, go for the 8- or maybe 7-iron. Shuffle your feet around to get to a good purchase in the sand but don't dig in too far

as it will restrict your swing.

Align the club face square to your target with the ball slightly back in your stance. This will help you to hit the ball first, before the sand, which is the object on this type of shot. Your feet and body lines should be slightly open though. With the ball being back in your stance the club face would tend to slice the ball as it hit it, so standing open will help you to compensate and hit it straight.

You might also find it helpful to grip

By only taking a three-quarter swing you will retain your balance more and hit the ball cleanly.

down on the club a little more than normal, for extra control. It also helps you to take the ball first, rather than digging into the sand.

Hover the club face above the sand, about level with the equator or top half of the ball. I find it useful to stand a little knock-kneed for this shot; that assists your balance and helps you to remain balanced through the swing.

It is important that you do not try to swing too hard or too fast as that will just result in your sliding and losing balance. As with most bunker shots the slow, three-quarter swing is the one to use.

Your aim is to pick the ball off cleanly, though you must avoid the temptation to scoop it off the surface of the sand without touching the sand. That will probably result in you topping the ball. Although that could still get the ball out of the bunker it is not the ideal shot.

You want to hit the ball cleanly, then to follow through into the sand. With your weight a little forward and staying there throughout the swing, and your wrists

A three-quarter swing will get enough power on the ball without causing you to lose your balance.

pre-cocked (automatically by the way you are standing - don't try to do it) you are promoting a more downward strike into the back of the ball. This set up will help you to hit the ball first. Please don't forget to rake the bunker as it's no fun having to play out of someone else's footprints. It is best to leave the rake *in* the bunker, not outside it.

You should also carefully read the rules concerning loose impediments and other items you might find in bunkers, as not everything can be removed.

Below: Most golfers are scared of playing from bunkers. That is the biggest single reason they fail to get the ball out. Play sensibly, swing smoothly and hit through the shot to ensure the ball flies out on a cushion of sand.

Trouble Shots

Sloping lies, rough, trees and playing in wind

Sloping lies

Golf is a strange game. The average golfer, once he or she has attained a reasonable level of competence, has little trouble hitting shots from a flat fairway, yet the moment the ball is sitting on a slope problems arise. Many players get themselves into a real pickle when it comes to hitting a ball off an up-slope, a down-slope or worse, a steep side lie.

The thing to remember is that, with just a slight variation, hitting a ball off a slope is the same as hitting one from a flat part of the fairway. All you need do is rely on Nature.

Uphill lies

I will deal first with the situation where you are climbing a fairly steep hill to the green, so the ball will be on an up-slope as you address it.

When you line up to the ball on the flat part of the fairway you stand square to the target and your shoulders are almost horizontal. For the moment ignore the fact that, as you address the ball, with the

On an up-slope your shoulders should be parallel to the slope itself, your weight more on your lower foot.

left hand lower on the club than the right, your left shoulder is slightly lower. On a slope you need to recreate that same position as closely as possible, rather than trying to get your body into some unnatural position.

For a moment, forget about golf. Walk up a slope and then turn sideways on, as you would to address a golf ball in this position. Don't even hold a club but just stand there. You should notice, straight away, that you have automatically altered your weight to support you on the slope, the left leg (lower down the slope) taking more weight than the right leg (higher up the slope). Nature has adjusted you and you did not even have to think about it.

If you look carefully at your position you should also notice that your left shoulder is lower than the right; again, this is a natural adjustment and you have not done it consciously.

When hitting uphill close your stance a little as the swing arc brings the club face into the ball slightly open.

Think back now to the shot from the flat fairway. You set up level with the terrain. Do the same on a sloping lie. With your back foot (left in this instance) taking more of the weight, your shoulders should automatically follow the line of the slope. Check it by doing what I have, using the club across the chest to show that you are in the right position.

Swinging a club on a slope is far more likely to pull you off balance than would be the case on a level surface, so you must be looking to swing more with your shoulders and arms, keeping the lower part of your body relatively still. Inevitably this means that a shorter club is more appropriate, even though the distance to your target may suggest a long club is needed. Only a very accomplished player can hit a long iron off a steeply sloping uphill lie and I would never recommend it.

You do, though, need to bear in mind that from an uphill lie the ball will rise faster, so if you are hitting a short shot a specific distance, you will need to take more club than on a flat surface. Because of the slope an 8-iron, for example, would take on the loft characteristics of a 9-iron or even a wedge. However, although you are going uphill and thus fighting gravity, don't try to hit harder, hit smoother!

I would also strongly advise you never to use a wooden club, not just because the shaft is longer than most irons, but also because a wood needs sweeping off the

On a slope you use your shoulders and arms more to swing, your feet staying fairly quiet to maintain your balance. Swing smoothly, sweeping the ball away. Never try to hit too hard.

turf. An iron shot is hit with more of a descending blow. With the wood your swing would reach its nadir too early, well behind the ball and you then risk thinning the ball.

On a shot from a level fairway you swing well back, turning your shoulders and hips on the back swing; then, coming down into the ball your hips turn and move laterally through the ball, getting power into the shot. On a severe slope you would lose balance if you did that, so just take a three-quarter swing with your arms and shoulders, keeping your right foot firmly planted on the ground. Your weight is already on your left foot so there is no weight transfer to take place in the back swing.

As you swing through the ball it is impossible to move your hips laterally as that would only pull you out of position as your weight would either topple left as your hips tried to move, or you would lower your body relative to the slope and hit too far behind the ball, what is known as a "fat" shot.

The ball should be in the middle of the stance and you should be standing very slightly closed to the target, if anything, because you hit the ball with your hands slightly behind the club head rather than pulling them through as you normally do. Much of this is perfectly natural, though, and not something about which you should be conscious.

If you remember to set your body parallel to the slope, swing slow and only three-quarters length, using a shorter club to just move the ball up the fairway, you won't go far wrong.

Downhill lies

Of course, what goes up must come down, so at some stage on this hilly course you will be faced with a downhill lie, and here the same thing applies, again with one slight variation.

Because you are going downhill, the ball will fly lower than normal and therefore will go further - it will also be helped on its way by gravity. You will need, therefore, less club than normal for the distance you have, using a 7-iron in place of a 5-iron, for example.

You should also set up slightly open, but again with the ball in the middle of your stance. Set your weight firmly where nature places it, on the lower (front) foot, your shoulders matching the slope. Again, take only a three-quarters swing and use your shoulders and arms, keeping your lower body still in the back swing.

On the follow through it is quite likely that you will lose your balance as you hit through the ball and topple forwards toward the target. That will do no damage to the shot and, particularly on a steep slope, is almost inevitable, so don't let it worry you. Up to the point of impact, though, you should maintain your balance as perfectly as you can.

When you are hitting a ball downhill to

Again, let Nature dictate your stance, with your shoulders parallel to the slope.

a green some distance away you might be tempted to think you can safely reach the green. In many cases you can, but a word of warning. If there is a bunker or some other hazard in front of the green it will be almost impossible to get the ball to rise sufficiently to carry it and then to stop on the green. Your only sensible option (and this is what golf is all about!) is to hit something like a 9-iron forward to safety and then pitch over the problem.

Don't try to be a hero and don't try trick shots. They don't work on a sufficiently regular basis for you to be sure that you can avoid wasting a shot.

If you have a downhill shot to a green fairly close then of course you can use the option of getting the ball up and over any hazard, landing it safely on the green. Remember only to swing slowly and smoothly, and to use less club than you normally would for this distance: thus, for a 7-iron distance, use an 8- or 9-iron. At all costs avoid trying to scoop the ball up in the air as that will almost inevitably result in a thinned shot.

Because of the swing arc the club comes into the ball slightly closed so offset this by standing a little open on a downhill slope.

On the back swing you want to maintain your balance so swing more with the arms, keeping the lower body fairly quiet. This is why a three-quarter swing is all you need.

Side lies

Side lies are always difficult, but again I would suggest that you let Nature do her work. Our first situation is with the ball above your feet.

Walk up a steep hill and what happens? Your body adjusts itself, just like a spirit level, so that you are, in relation to the

With the ball above your feet you need to aim left as the ball will follow gravity and the slope.

Again you must maintain your balance so no more than a three-quarter swing.

slope, leaning forward, though in reality you are just remaining upright. If you leaned back so that you were at right angles to the slope you would fall over backwards. You are almost balancing on your toes to stay upright and your back is fairly straight. Do exactly the same when you are on the golf course and have this type of lie.

On a side lie, with the ball above your feet, you stand just as you would if walking up the hill, or merely standing still.

Your feet might be slightly wider apart than normal, to help you balance and, because the ball has come up to meet you, you only need a short club. It will help if you grip down further on that as well. Once again this is a shoulders and arms swing, only three-quarters at the most, with little lower body movement.

Now let's think about alignment. If you stand on a side slope and roll a ball, where does it go? Down the slope, of

A less than full back swing means the same on the follow through; keep your balance.

course. Thus any shot you hit will do the same; it will follow the slope and gravity. From our position here, the ball will hook. It is inevitable. To counteract this, what you must do is to aim the ball higher up the slope, in effect trying to hit it left of whatever the target may be.

Yet you must be careful, for as you swing a club into a slope the toe of the club will hit the ground first. That could cause the club to swing even more open and could result in a push left or a shank. This, again, is one more reason to swing slowly and smoothly.

The other major problem lie is the one where you are standing on a side slope with the ball below your feet. Here again your body will automatically adjust itself so that you are almost sitting back on your heels, your knees bent forward to keep your spine upright. If you stood at right angles to the slope you would fall forwards.

This time a slightly longer club might be needed as the ball is, relatively, further from you. It will, though, again, follow gravity and the slope so is likely to slice left. You therefore need to be aiming right of your target to compensate.

On the previous slope we saw that the toe of the club would hit the ground first. Here the opposite happens, with the heel making contact first and forcing the club face closed.

On all slopes you will see that the object is to be balanced, to swing slowly and smoothly and to play safe. Get the ball back into the middle of the fairway for your next shot. Remember, on the golf course you cannot save shots - you can only avoid wasting them.

Above: With the ball below your feet aim right, higher up the slope as the ball will again follow gravity.
Above Right: To get closer to the ball crouch more with your knees more flexed. Never bend over from the waist.
Below Right: Again, keep your balance by only swinging three quarter length.

A shot across water

Many golfers, particularly those who are relative newcomers to the game, have a great fear of hitting the ball over water, or a bunker for that matter. Give someone a shot of 90 yards across a lush fairway to a green and they will do it every time.

Set up with your hands ahead of the ball and the ball slightly back in your stance.

Change the fairway to water and most golfers' knees turn to jelly.

Replace that lush green fairway with water and it immediately becomes a completely different matter altogether. Why?

Without wishing to be accused of plagiarism, I would suggest you remember the title of a very good novel by a famous author, who said that *fear is the key*.

What can you do to alleviate this fear? The first thing I would ask is: if you lose the ball in the water, will it cause you financial distress, or is it your last ball? If your financial position can stand the loss of one golf ball, or if you have another couple in your golf bag, then what are you worrying about?

When you hit a normal shot across that lush fairway the loft on the club face gets the ball up into the air. You don't try to scoop it up; you don't worry about it landing on that fairway.

Because the hands are ahead of the ball at address the wrists are already slightly cocked. Swing up to three-quarters and maintain that wrist angle.

The club then accelerates down into the back of the ball and will hit it smoothly and cleanly. Don't try to scoop it up and don't try to hit any differently from normal. Relax and just think of the cost of a new golf ball. If you can't afford it give up golf!

It is exactly the same with a shot across water. You must ensure that you have enough club to carry the distance and if you want to make absolutely certain that you hit the ball up, have the ball in the middle of your stance but a little more weight on your right side, so that you are leaning slightly more towards the target.

That will virtually guarantee that you will hit the ball a descending blow. The club face gets the ball airborne, you don't have to try to scoop it up. Just hit it at your normal pace, not trying to hit it any harder than usual. It really is that easy.

This is more of an arms and shoulders shot with little lower body or leg movement. You do, though, follow through just as normal, because the speed of the club at impact will pull your body through. Never try to stop the club and never try to stab at the ball.

Shots from the rough

Every golf course has areas of rough just off the fairway. Depending on the time of year and the course, this rough may be light and fluffy, or deep and nasty.

Being able to play the ball from it is essential for every golfer. Your first aim, as for bunker shots, is to get the ball back in play first time, every time. Far too often I see inexperienced golfers trying to hit impossible shots from deep rough with the inevitable result that the ball goes nowhere.

When you are in the rough your first priority is to get out. Look carefully at your options rather than just going in and flailing at the ball.

You should be out on the fairway looking for the ideal spot from where you would most like to play your next shot, but be realistic. Often, your best option is to come out sideways, gaining little distance. Sometimes you may even have to hit backwards towards the tee to reach safety.

You must, though, ocasionally swallow your pride and hit the simple shot that will get the ball back on the fairway.

Your best friend in deep rough is the sand wedge which will dig its way

73

through most of the undergrowth and splash the ball back onto the fairway. It also has the advantage of being the shortest club in the bag, which can be useful when you are in amongst the foliage and perhaps bushes.

Set up with the ball off your right instep as you would for a bunker shot and do exactly the same. Take a three-quarter swing and really hit through the ball; you must never stab at it.

I suggest you take a few practice swings first, well away from the ball but in similar conditions, to establish whether the club will cut through the undergrowth or not.

Hit through the ball as hard as you can, obviously taking into account where you want to land it.

By standing with your hands slightly ahead of the ball you promote a descending blow into the back of the ball. The loft on the club face will get it out, but you must hit hard.

Take a couple of practice swings first to make sure the club will cut through the undergrowth.

Of course not all rough is deep. Just off the edge of the fairway you are likely to encounter the semi-rough which, providing your ball is sitting up and not buried in a divot, can give you a very good opportunity to get the ball to the green, if it is within reach.

A fairway wood can be the ideal tool to use in these circumstances if you are faced with a long shot as a wood sweeps the ball away, unlike an iron which hits

In light rough if the ball is sitting up you may find a fairway wood better to use as it will result in a firmer contact with the ball.

the type of shot which produces a divot. In fact, if the ball is sitting up an iron could hit too much underneath it and sky the ball, greatly reducing the distance you will hit it.

If you are taking a wood, set up with the ball slightly forward in your stance, your feet and shoulders square to your target. Beware of any overhanging branches which may be between you and the target and which could deflect the ball. Hit it smoothly and straight. With the loft of a 3-wood it should come out fairly low and fly well to the target. You must, though, make sure it does rise in the air as you can't run this type of shot along the ground.

If you are closer to the green you should use an iron though remember two things; first, a ball sitting up will travel less distance, so you need to be very sure that you don't leave the ball short by hitting too much underneath it. That has the same effect as hitting a short iron from a tee peg; the ball will rise higher but travel less distance.

Secondly, once grass gets between the club and ball it is impossible to apply backspin and the ball may roll further than you want once it lands. This is often the case if the ball is sitting down in the grass.

There is one very awkward situation that you are bound to encounter on the golf course and which causes so many golfers problems.

As always a very simple little tip will help you and it is virtually the same as for that little pitch across the bunker earlier.

Round most greens there is an area of semi rough which you could be in if you miss the green. You are often faced with a shot of no more than twenty yards to the pin. Just remember to keep your hands ahead of the ball at address and the wrists are already cocked. Keep them that way throughout the swing, remembering to follow through, so that the club is not slowing down as it hits the ball.

Trees

Virtually all golf courses have trees, only true links courses like the famous Old Course at St Andrews not having them.

At some stage you will, undoubtedly, find your view of the green blocked by at least one and you then have the problem

Hands ahead of the ball, weight well forward, keep the wrists cocked and hit through the ball.

Do make sure that you are far enough from the tree and have enough loft on the club to get the ball over the top, rather than hitting the higher branches and deflecting the ball.

Always check that you can swing the club freely without getting caught up in overhanging branches.

of getting the ball over, round, or under them. Which route you take will depend upon how far you have to go to the green, how far from the tree you are, and how big the tree is.

We are going to look at the three main shots you will need to know; how to get over the tree, how to get round it and how to keep the ball low so that it goes under any overhanging branches.

There are also occasions when you might have to take a shot from almost under a tree and have a restricted back swing. In those circumstances choose your shot carefully and then, before you attempt it, have a few practice swings with the club to make sure your back swing is not hindered by any overhanging branches. Try to do this as close to the ball as possible (being very careful not to touch the ball of course) and very slowly, watching the top of the back swing. But do bear in mind that on the real swing you will swing further back than when you do it in slow motion, so make allowances for this.

The next problem is getting the ball over a tree if it is directly in your way. I would urge you, before you play this shot, to look carefully at any alternatives. You may find that your best option will be to go round rather than over. Think about it before you do it.

You will need a club that will get enough height on the ball to hit it safely over the top of the tree, even if you very slightly mis-hit it. You must, therefore, be far enough back from the tree to be able to do this.

The next problem is that, if you are going for height you will not get too much distance. After all, you can't hit a 3-wood over a tall tree just in front of you! The main fault of less experienced players in this situation is rather like that when they play over a lake. In trying to scoop the ball up extra high they top it, hitting it lower.

Address the ball a little to the front of your stance, your weight and hands pushing ahead of the ball. Maintain that position and hit down hard.

You should address the ball slightly forward of centre in your stance, your weight favouring your right side so that your hands are ahead of the ball. Make a full back swing and hit down hard, but smoothly into the back of the ball. With this shot as with all others you must never try to swing faster, just swing the club smoother.

When you want to keep the ball low you should play it centrally in your stance and use a straighter faced club, though you can achieve the same effect by hooding the club face, pushing your hands forward more. Never close the club face, keep it square to the target. Your 3-wood could be ideal for this shot if you have some distance to go.

If you are close to the green and need to keep the ball low do exactly the same, with the ball a touch further back in your stance. As you swing through keep your

To keep the ball low use a straighter faced club or hood the face. Again, swing smoothly.

with the ball a touch further back in your stance. As you swing through keep your hands held firm rather than releasing them, rather as we did when playing the short shot over the bunker much earlier. The photograph below shows how you should finish this shot to get the ball out of trouble but keep it low.

You must not, though, decelerate the club as it approaches the ball; again we come back to the fault of stabbing at the ball rather than hitting through it.

To keep the ball low don't release the hands as you come through the ball. Keep the wrists firm, but make sure you hit hard through the impact zone.

To fade, or slice the ball, from right to left, stand with an open stance, the ball forward in your stance. Aim the club at the first target and let the slice bring it round in mid-air to the real target.

You must always go through the ball.

Now for those shots where we need to move the ball round the tree. This brings us to the art of shaping the shot, which is also dealt with briefly in the lesson on driving. It is the same principle.

You stand with the ball fairly forward in your stance and with an open stance, your feet and shoulders aiming right of the first target. On a shot which you need to shape you must have two targets. The first is the direction in which you want the ball to start. Your second target is the real target, the green perhaps.

Aim the club face squarely at the first target, which should safely clear the tree. Your open stance will then help to turn the ball in mid-air.

It must be mentioned that it is easier to fade the ball on a longer shot than one with a short iron.

Finally, the shot which needs to be drawn or hooked round a tree. For this, the opposite applies from the previous shot.

Stand with the club face square to your first target, which will safely clear the tree, but with a closed stance, the ball slightly back of centre of your stance. Once again swing smoothly; your speed and rhythm should be the same on every single shot, and nobody has ever swung the golf club too slowly.

All these shots need practising and it should be your aim, at the practice or the driving range, to learn to shape your shots at will. You never know when you might need them!

Above Right: To fade the ball have it forward in your stance and stand open to the target. The club face must be square to the first target.

Below Right: To draw the ball have it back in your stance and stand closed to the target. Again the club face must be square to your first target.

Playing in wind

Unless you are very lucky you will find yourself playing in windy conditions from time to time.

Many people find this disconcerting and, particularly if they are hitting into the wind, feel that they have to hit the ball harder to get it the same distance as on a still day.

A golf ball hit into the wind will rise and spin back if hit too hard and with too much backspin. If hit with topspin it will travel further and stay lower.

Hitting the ball really hard with a short club is likely to hit it higher, where the wind affects it more and it loses distance.

Hitting a ball with a straight faced club (a driver is the best) will keep it low and long into the wind.

You can help it by having the ball slightly further back in your stance than normal and by moving your body across the ball slightly faster as you swing the club, but this does not mean swinging faster. The great Tommy Armour once said, "when it's breezy, swing it easy."

There will, though, be occasions when you want to use a headwind to your advantage, if, for example, you are hitting to a green and want to stop the ball very quickly. On such occasions take one more club than you think necessary for the dis-

"When it's breezy, swing it easy."

tance and hit it hard. The ball will rise and, buffeted by the wind, should drop almost vertically. Of course it depends on the strength of the wind and you must beware of cross winds which can blow the ball off line. The same applies to any normal shots where you have a cross wind. Always remember that a cross wind is at leat 50% against you, so it will slow the ball unless you bore it low into the wind.

Finally, never forget that a strong wind can affect a putt as much as a drive, so allow a little for it.

Putting

Putting

When you are on a sloping green it is fairly obvious that you must aim to one side of the hole so that the ball will roll down the slope and hopefully into the hole.

Putting is the most individual part of the game, yet also one of the most important. Looking at an average par-72 course, putting should account for 36 strokes, exactly half of your round. If you get round in 36 putts you are doing pretty well. Sadly, many players take far more and it is this that partly ruins their score. If you could walk off the course having just double putted every green you would probably reduce your handicap by five or six shots.

In the professional game every golfer is looking for single putts virtually every time. Of course, having a very sharp short game will help enormously as you are often then able to get the ball onto the green within single putting distance with your approach shot.

I would say that, in general, you should be looking to single putt any ball within four feet of the hole. Most professionals would feel unhappy if they failed to hole out from twelve feet on a flat green.

Most people miss putts because they fail to line up correctly. Whenever I play in pro-ams I see, time and time again, carelessness on the greens where, with correct alignment and just a little more attention to detail, the average player could always hole out in regulation.

The first thing you must do on the green is to "read" the gradient. Is there a slope: and if so, which way does it go? You will normally see professionals "plumb-bobbing" with their putter to understand the slope of the green. They do this by standing (or crouching) behind the ball, holding the putter by the grip but letting it hang freely. If you then move so that the putter shaft obscures the ball and part of the hole, you will be able to tell if the hole is cut on a slope.

If you can see more of the hole to the left of the shaft, the green slopes right to left as you look at it and you need to hit your putt to a point right of the hole. If there is more of the hole to the right of the shaft the opposite is true.

Plumb bobbing can help you to see if the hole is cut on a slope. Take care and understand the amount of borrow.

There may be times when the shaft covers the centre of the hole but you can still see that the hole is not on level ground. Take note carefully of the slope and choose the spot at which you must roll the ball first if it is to follow gravity and run down the slope to the hole.

No book can teach you this exactly; it is something you must experience for yourself and practise constantly. The other major problem is that of under-hitting the ball on a putt. The main difference between club golfers and professionals is that the former normally leave the ball short of the hole; professionals normally leave it beyond the hole. Some people say that the only time you might want to leave the ball short of the hole is if you are putting uphill.

However, I have to ask: why do you want to leave the ball short? Surely the best thing to do is to get the ball **in** the hole. Make sure you stroke the ball well enough that it will have sufficient speed to reach the hole and drop. If it does go past you have an even better opportunity to hole it coming back as you will have seen it roll and should know which way the slope goes.

The most commonly used putting grip is the reverse overlap, which is the same as the Vardon grip used in the rest of the game with one tiny alteration. The small finger of the left hand, which normally rests on top of the index finger of the right hand, changes places with it, hence the name of reverse overlap. Having the index finger of the right hand overlapping the left will help you balance the putter better.

I mentioned earlier that the most common problem on the putting green was lack of correct alignment of the putter head. Having aligned that perfectly square to your target, but keep in mind that the target might not be the hole itself if the green slopes, you next need to align your body. It is fairly common, and much easier, to stand with your feet slightly open to the line of the putt. On a full swing with any other club your hips turn and move laterally on the down swing, "clearing" to give enough room for the arms to swing the club down unhindered.

On a putt there is virtually no lower

Above Right: The reverse overlap grip is the most popular for putting. The index finger of the right hand and the little finger of the left hand change places.

Below Right: Alignment of the putter head is vital if you are to hit the putt at your target. Many putters have a small mark on the top to help you.

body movement so you need to get the hips out of the way to begin with. Standing slightly open to the target helps you to do this.

There is another benefit in standing with an open stance. You will remember from the lesson on the short game that the swing goes back 40%, through 60%. It's the same with putting. The open stance restricts the back swing. However, although your feet are slightly open to the target, your shoulders **must be parallel to the target.**

The putting stroke is a shoulders movement only. You should consider the shoulders, arms and putter as a single unit, a large "Y". It is almost like a large pendulum which just rocks from side to side. Standing with your hands together in front of you, but not holding the putter, just rock your shoulders up and down. Your hands gently swing from side to side. This is the correct feel of the putting motion and one you should feel every time you putt.

There is a tendency among some golfers to use the wrists too much in putting. Unlike our full swing where the wrists are such a vital factor in the production of extra power, on a putt we are looking for deadly accuracy and feel. The wrists remain static, holding the putter firm throughout the short swing and it is only the shoulders which rock from side to side.

The putter head does move back inside the line on the back swing, so don't try to hold it straight artificially. If you do that you may well take the putter outside the line and be cutting across the ball as you hit it. Don't forget the 40:60 ratio; you need to follow through after you have hit the ball, with the feeling that you are brushing the ball towards the hole. Never quit on a putt and never just stab at the

When putting you should stand with your feet slightly open but you must have your shoulders parallel to the ball to target line.

ball. The putter head should, on all but the shortest of putts, finish pointing well towards its target.

Putting is something you really must

On a putt your wrists must stay firm, the only movement being the pendulum motion of the "Y" formed by your shoulders, arms and putter. You can clearly see this motion in the pictures below, left and right. Keep your head still, too, until you have struck the ball, and follow through. The putter head must finish pointing towards the target.

practise often. Professionals spend so much time practising their putting skills. Quite often I will spend an entire day just practising my putting and although I know few people will have the time to do the same, you should try to spend a good percentage of your practice time honing your putting skills. On the page opposite there are some putting skills practice routines which will help you, but remember, you can practise putting at home on those dark winter evenings. All you need is a fairly flat carpet (preferably not deep pile) and a clear target, which can be almost

anything; an upturned tee-peg or another golf ball are ideal.

Every professional, when away on Tour, spends half the evening in his hotel bedroom putting along the carpet once it's dark outside. You can do it, too, just for fifteen minutes or so. You will see the difference, I promise you.

Finally, before we leave the putting green I would aks you to repair all pitch marks. It only takes a couple of seconds

Below: From about three feet try to hole twenty balls. If you miss one, start again.

and helps to keep the greens in a decent condition, for your benefit and that of others.

With a pitch mark repair fork, gently push the displaced turf back into the middle of the mark, rather than lifting it from underneath. Then carefully tap the surface down level with your putter head. You should try to repair your own pitch mark and at least two others, on every green. A pitch mark left unrepaired for fifteen minutes will take two weeks to "heal". Please do it, as it makes putting that much easier. Thank you.

Left: With three (or more) balls in a line at different distances from the hole try to hole them all. Begin at just one foot, then two feet, three and so on. See how far out you can get. If you miss, go back to the beginning.

Below: Use a circle of balls around the hole and try to hole them all. This will help you particularly if you can find a practice green with a slope.

Driving

and the long shots

Driving

Look carefully at the hole and see whether a fade or draw might be better than a straight shot. Keep the ball away from trouble if you can.

Every golfer wants to be able to drive the ball long distances and, whilst it is important, if you are to reach the green in two shots on most par-4s, to be able to hit a realistic distance, you should not sacrifice any direction just to get the ball further. After all, if you are long but wayward you risk ending up much further off the fairway than someone who is straighter but perhaps shorter off the tee.

You must, therefore, ensure you can regularly hit the ball straight, or at least towards a definite target, for not every shot should be straight. Indeed, it is the ability of professionals to be able to work the ball from side to side at will that sets them apart from the average club golfer. Many fairways have trouble on one side and the professional is looking to work the ball toward the green with the least possible risk. That may mean hitting a draw or a fade to keep the ball away from trouble, rather than a very straight shot.

You will find, when you play golf regularly, that your shots have a certain shape about them. Some people cannot avoid fading the ball (slicing is an exaggerated fade and can be cured relatively easily),

whilst others are habitual hookers of the ball, always pulling it round left to right in the air, though with some control this becomes a draw, one of the best shots you can play and the one preferred by most professionals as it gives more distance and control.

If you can only hit a fade, or a draw, you should consider using it to your advantage, aiming the ball to the appropriate side, knowing that it will move round in mid-air to land approximately where you want it. However, it will pay you dividends to work on your game so that you become capable of fading or drawing the ball at will, as well as being able to hit the ball high or low off the tee, to take advantage of, or avoid, strong winds. We shall come on to the various shapes of shot in a while, but let's deal, first of all, with the long, straight drive.

Many books suggest you should hit a 3-wood or a 5-wood from the tee. Whilst there are occasions when either of these could be the right club, I am going to teach you how to hit the ball confidently with your driver.

The thing to remember about this club is that the swing is no different to any other shot - with the exception of the very short irons. Many golfers, particularly those relatively new to the game, have a fear of taking the driver out of the bag, partly, I suspect, because the shots they have hit with that club have been somewhat wayward and unpredictable. Once you become confident of your ability with the driver it will quickly become one of your favourite clubs.

Drivers, and all the woods for that matter, often come with the set of irons you buy, but you can easily change them if you prefer. When buying a set of irons that suit you, look carefully at the woods to see if they suit your type of swing. Metal woods are now very popular and do help with distance, though a good

The swing with the driver is no different from that with a 9-iron.

player might well find that a persimmon wood will give better control as the ball is on the club face a split second longer than on a metal wood. The average club golfer will find, though, that this does not affect him or her and a metal wood might be the best choice, though it is a matter of personal preference.

Don't just buy the three woods which come with the set of irons; they are normally priced separately anyway, so you can buy any woods you want. Go for something you feel comfortable with, rather than just buying a label.

Graphite shafts could well help the shorter hitters, adding ten yards or maybe more to each shot, as the graphite shafts tend to be lighter and thus produce more club head speed at impact, if swung properly! Longer hitters, though, often find the graphite shafts too flexible with a resultant loss of control, particularly in

Never tee the ball too high. You can see here that the top of the driver is level with the equator of the ball.

strong wind. Either a stiffer graphite or a steel shaft could be the answer, though again you really should try clubs before buying them. This holds good especially for drivers which can be very expensive.

We shall begin by hitting straight shots with the driver. One of the biggest faults I see in pro-ams is the tendency to tee the ball too high. This may surprise some of you who think the ball should be sitting right up. It has long been taught that a ball teed high will draw, one teed low will fade. That is true only in the extreme, as you can tell if you use the driver from

a tight lie on the fairway. Inevitably it will fade, which can be very useful at times when you want a long, low fade.

As the photograph on the previous page shows, the top of the club should be level with the equator of the ball at most. The ball should be no higher than this. This will not cause a slice if you square the club face to the ball at impact and swing the driver with a good, sweeping motion.

Having teed the ball the next step is to go through your pre-shot routine, first identifying a real target on the fairway and then aligning the club face and your body square to that target. Too many golfers spoil their chance of hitting a good tee shot by failing to choose a definable target, or target area.

With a short shot to the green you have a clearly identifiable target, the pin. When you are hitting over 200 yards down a fairway there is not such an identifiable target so you need to find one and focus on it. It might be a light patch of grass opposite a tree, or just beyond a bunker; it

Never forget your pre-shot routine. Do it every time.

Always choose a real target that you can see and can reach.

might be just over, or short of, a stream crossing the fairway. Whatever it is, find it and focus on it. Never just hit aimlessly, not even when just practising at the course or driving range. Of course you must find a target that is within your reach, or just beyond it. Don't be over-ambitious, yet try to stretch yourself just a little each time. That way you will build up your confidence and your power.

Having found that target stand behind the ball and check for an intermediate target a couple of feet in front of the ball to help you align your club face, then your feet and shoulders before taking your grip.

The ball should be fairly well forward in your stance. Begin with your feet together, the ball in the middle of your stance. Take a small sideways step with your right foot so that the ball is just inside the heel as you look at it head-on; then a larger side-step with your left foot, to give you sufficient balance. Ideally your feet should be about shoulder width apart.

Your posture needs to be athletic and flexed, not wooden. It helps enormously to bend your knees slightly, keeping your spine straight as you bend from the hips, not the waist. At this point you should be

The ball should be fairly well forward in your stance and you must remain poised with your feet and shoulders perfectly aligned to the target.

able to see a direct line down from each shoulder to about your knees. Check this by holding a club against one shoulder. It should be hanging very close to your knee, though don't get yourself into an uncomfortable position. If the club hangs too far in front of your knee, try flexing your knees a little more, as well as checking that your spine is reasonably straight and that you are not hunched over. It will help with your swing.

At address you should have an almost vertical line from your right shoulder to your knee. Check this with a club.

As you now get ready to swing you should have a "swing thought" in your head. You have chosen your target and that stays in your mind, but you also need to be thinking about swinging smoothly to get the ball down the fairway towards your target. Never just think about trying to hit the ball a long way. If you take away your swing thoughts you are likely to mis-hit the ball.

You may have read books or been told to keep your head still during the swing. Whilst true, I would like to introduce you to a new idea. When you swing, your shoulders turn through 90° and it is physically impossible to keep your head absolutely still. Thinking about keeping your head still whilst you swing just increases the pressure on yourself because it is something else to think about.

Instead, just keep one eye focused on the back of the ball. Obviously, if you turn correctly your head will not move out of position by more than a couple of inches, but focusing one eye on the ball is a physical act and it is easier to do something physical than mental.

If you look carefully at the photographs of the swing sequence (see pages 103-105) when I am driving you will see that my head does, in fact, move an inch or so on the back swing. It's almost impossible to stop it without interrupting the rhythm of the swing and you must remember that the golf swing is an athletic movement which needs to flow naturally and smoothly. Keep a smooth rhythm.

At the top of the back swing your shoulders should have turned through 90° and you should still be able to see a direct line between your right shoulder and right knee. Get a friend to hold a club against your right shoulder and let it hang loose. You can check, using this method, whether you have swayed on the turn or whether you have dipped forward too much.

At the top of the back swing too, there should be a vertical line from your right shoulder to your knee.

Power

Everybody wants to know the secret of power in driving. There really is no secret. You will see, as you read this, just how easy it can be to increase the distance you hit the ball, but I must warn you that not every golfer has the ability or strength in the wrists and forearms, for that is where much of the power is generated, to hit the ball long distances.

You will recall that, as the club is swung back and up the wrists will cock. As you begin the down swing and your hips turn and move laterally to the right, your hands are pulling down on the club. Looking very carefully at the swing sequence photographs you will see that, as the downswing begins, the angle between the arms and the club shaft is fairly acute. As the downswing continues this angle **does not alter.** When my arms have reached waist height on the way down that angle is still the same.

Now for the "secret", if there is one. At impact the wrists must have uncocked to replicate the address position. At address the wrists are holding the club just behind the ball and, because the club is hanging down, there is no angle between the right arm and shaft. You have to be back at this position at impact, or as near as makes no difference.

Going back to the downswing, at waist height there is still an angle between arms and club. Between that position and impact the wrists have to uncock and get the club face back to the square position, with the right arm and shaft forming a straight line. To do that takes what are often called "fast hands".

Between waist height and impact the club head has to be accelerated to catch up with the hands. Think about this very carefully. At waist height the hands are well ahead of the club head in the down-swing. At impact the club head must have caught up with the hands so that they are level, thus squaring the club face to the ball, the position we had at address.

Because the arms are moving fast (the entire swing takes just over one second from start to finish) the only parts of the body that can make the club head catch up with the arms are the hands, which are

At impact the club head is returned square to the ball, the hands having caught up with the club head.

Just after impact the hands release, but the straight arms show that the club head has been driven through the ball.

The left knee then kicks through as the arms continue swinging through impact, rather than hitting at the ball.

attached to the arms by the wrists. Thus the wrists have to uncock with sufficient speed and power to get the club head level with the arms.

It is the movement of uncocking the wrists as late as possible that creates the extra power in the golf swing. It is called "hitting late" and is the only way to generate the extra power that separates the good player from the average. To see whether you are hitting late will probably take a video camera and a slow motion

replay, but if you have access to a video camera, or maybe your club professional does, you will learn more about your swing in five minutes viewing than in a year on the practice range on your own.

Wrist and forearm strength does make a difference and it is very difficult for those with very weak wrists to create enough speed at this stage to get the club head back square at impact. Many women lack the physical strength to produce real power (this is not a criticism but just a comment) and thus swing more with their arms, getting the ball straight but not long. Build up your wrist strength if you want to be a good golfer. Try squeezing a squash ball for ten minutes a day, alternating between wrists, but don't do it before playing or it will take away much of the feel you need for short shots and putts. Ironically, when playing left handed your right wrist needs to be stronger.

By understanding the importance of the late hit you will go some way towards achieving extra distance, but a word of warning. You may find that if you deliberately try to keep the club head behind the hands as long as possible, you push the ball. This will occur if you delay the hit too long so that, at impact, the club head is still behind your hands, leaving the club face slightly open, or because you are bringing the club head into the ball at a slightly different angle, pushing the ball straight left. It might not be the only reason you are pushing or fading, though; check the static things first; the grip and alignment; if they are correct the answer probably lies in the area of the late hit. Whilst this book will help you to better understand your golf, a visit to your club professional, who can look at your swing and detect any faults very rapidly, will prove invaluable. This book is an addition to lessons from a professional, not an alternative.

The address with the 3-iron is virtually the same as for a 9-iron. Don't change your grip, the ball position or stance.

Long irons

More golfers have problems with long irons than with short irons. Why? Is it because the club shaft is longer; the loft on the club face much less; or because the ball has to be hit further?

I suppose it is really a combination of all three and certainly any problems in a golfer's technique will be exaggerated when using a long iron.

First, the club shaft. A 3-iron is several inches longer than a 9-iron, but as the photographs show the swing is exactly the same. Because the shaft of a 9-iron is shorter the club head is moving faster but you do not consciously swing faster with a 9-iron than a 3-iron. In fact the opposite is probably true - you try to swing faster with the 3-iron than the 9-iron. Logic will tell you that it is totally unnecessary. You should almost swing slower with the longer club!

The loft on longer irons is less than that on the short irons. The latter get the ball up in the air and safely down on the green, the former are made to hit further. Inevitably, that means they hit the ball lower. If you want the ball to climb very rapidly, use an 8-iron. If you want to hit it 170 yards, use a 4-iron. It will go lower

The swing with the 3-iron is the same as that with the 9-iron. Swing slowly.

and, because the ball hits the ground at a different angle, is more likely to run once it does land, giving you extra distance, whereas a ball coming down fast, as when you hit an 8-iron, will stop faster. The whole point of using long irons is to hit the ball reasonably long distances. Get it out of your mind that the ball will climb high; it's not meant to.

The grip and stance are exactly the same as for any other shot, the ball about midway between the centre of your stance and your right instep. The club is

swung, like the driver, fully and should be a slightly flat swing, but not that you have to worry about. Never stand there and think: "I must swing this one flat". The ball is swept away with only a small divot. Don't try to hit down into the back of the ball as you would a wedge; it's not a punch shot. With a short iron the divot tends to be fairly deep and long; with a long iron it should be short and shallow.

The same rule concerning the late hit applies as for the driver. As I have said, most problems with long irons are more in the head than anywhere else. Practise hitting long irons regularly.

You will sometimes want to hit a long iron from the tee as a number of par-3s are long enough to require a long iron or even a wood. The same rules apply. Align everything properly, keep one eye focused on the ball, swing smoothly and sweep the ball away, remembering that, if you want power, you must hit late, only uncocking the wrists at the last minute. I always use a tee-peg on every par-3, even if the shot is so short that it only needs a 6-iron. I must point out though that with a 6-iron off the tee you are not sweeping the ball but hitting down into the back of it, taking a full divot. Only with the long irons should you sweep the ball.

On the tee is the only time when you have the opportunity of giving yourself the perfect lie. Don't waste it.

Fairway woods

The 3- and 5-woods are made to be used from the fairway, where you want distance and loft on the ball, though there is nothing to stop you from using them off the tee in certain circumstances.

There really is no difference between the shots with the woods from the fairway than for any other shot, with the exception that the ball is swept away with virtually no divot, the club head just brushing the turf. To achieve this you need to possibly flex your knees a little more than normal, though don't overdo it. This will exaggerate the flatter swing and help keep the club head low for longer as it comes into the impact position. The ball is just forward of centre of your stance so that you catch it with the club head travelling straight along the ground rather than still coming down (as with a short iron) or rising (as with the driver off the tee).

Don't rush the shot, don't try to hit harder just because you want to send the ball further. The length of shaft and the club face will do the work. All you need do is to concentrate on swinging the club smoothly. Have that as your swing thought every time and I assure you, you **will** play better golf.

With a fairway wood your aim is to sweep the ball off the surface, without taking a divot. Swing slowly and smoothly and you might find it helpful to flex your knees a little more, which will force you to swing flatter.

The next three pages show the swing sequence with the driver, with some photographs from two angles. Study them carefully and learn to get yourself into similar positions, with the hands coming down ahead of the club head to help produce the power from the late hit. You must always remember to continue to hit through the ball, not just at it.

Above Left: From a good address position, the club is swung back by the shoulders rotating. Do not sway.

Below Left: Near the top of the back swing the shoulders have fully turned, winding up the power.

Above Right: The downswing begins with the hips turning and moving laterally ahead of the ball; notice, though, how far ahead of the club the hands are as they pull down.

Above Left: Just before impact and you can still see how the hands are ahead of the club head, pulling it through and creating the extra power.

Below Left: After impact the left arm has straightened as the club head is driven through impact. There is no deceleration here. At this point the head is still above the body pivot.

Above Right: Towards the full finish and the body has turned to face the target, the left knee having kicked round.

The swing from down the line.

Above Left: Note how the club is drawn back by the shoulders beginning to turn. There is no attempt at picking the club up.

Above Right: At the top of the back swing the shoulders have turned through 90° but the head has remained in place above the body's pivot.

Below Right: Through impact the body has maintained its shape, the arms have swung on a large arc building up power and the left knee is kicking towards the target.

Strategy
and concentration on the course

Strategy on the course

Having learnt how to hit a golf ball the next thing to do is to go and play a golf course. Sadly, this is where many golfers let themselves down.

Golf is a little like chess, you need to plan a couple of moves ahead. Many top professionals suggest you should play golf from the pin back to the tee, deciding first which side of the green you wish to putt from, then deciding from where you want to hit your approach shot. That, then, gives you the target for your tee shot. Whilst this is an over-simplification, and is only possible on a golf course you know well (including the pin position), it does have more than a grain of truth to it.

We have seen earlier that you should have a definite target on every shot, from the final putt, where the target is the hole, to the tee shot, where you need to be

Plan your way carefully. On this par-4, the 18th at The Belfry, home of the Ryder Cup in 1985, 1989 and 1993, the average golfer would have difficulty clearing the lake with his second shot. The tee shot should thus be hit straight with the second being an easy lay-up, using perhaps a 9-iron.

This then leaves an easy pitch across the lake to the heart of the green to leave either a single putt or a safe five, which is no embarrassment on this hole.

Only the longer hitters could attempt a long fade off the tee to leave a medium iron to the green for a par attempt.

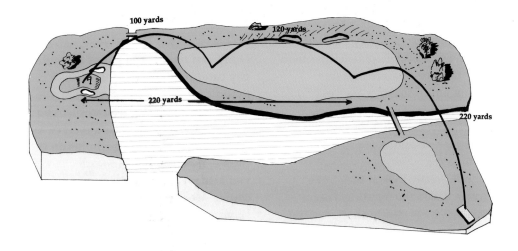

looking to land the ball well away from any potential hazards. The designers of golf courses often place a bunker or lake in exactly the spot from which you would most like to hit your next shot, of course, as this is part of their art, but you have to be able to manoeuvre the ball safely from tee to green, avoiding the hazards on the way.

Similarly, around the green you may well be faced with a short shot over a bunker. If you are nervous about playing such a shot, as well as still nervous about your bunker play, the sensible option might be to play a shot to another part of the green, probably leaving yourself with only a single putt for par. However, if you have a medium or high handicap the chances are you receive a stroke on the hole and can thus safely take two putts for a net par.

More importantly, the ball will be safely on the putting surface so you have no sand to worry about. Golf is a game where the easy option is almost always the sensible one. Always play the shot you know you can safely play, rather than going for the once-in-a-lifetime shot.

One thing which many golfers overlook is the stroke index of each hole. The majority of players get onto a tee, look at the par of the hole and then just line up for their tee shot.

You should really look at the stroke index (often called the handicap) of the hole. This is always clearly shown on the scorecard and normally on the tee itself. Whilst you should always be aiming to improve your scores and lower your handicap, playing each hole according to

FERNDOWN GOLF CLUB Scorecard					
				Score	
Hole	Yds.	Par	S.I.	A	B
1	399	4	13		
2	175	3	17		
3	399	4	3		
4	398	4	11		
5	208	3	9		
6	411	4	1		
7	480	5	7		
8	303	4	15		
9	430	4	5		
Out	3203	35			
10	487	5	10		
11	440	4	2		
12	187	3	12		
13	489	5	6		
14	158	3	18		
15	397	4	4		
16	305	4	16		
17	397	4	8		
18	403	4	14		
In	3263	36			
Total	6466	71			

Don't just look at the par of the hole, pay careful attention to the stroke index (handicap). This shows whether you receive a stroke. If, for example, you have a handicap of 14, you receive a stroke on fourteen of the holes on the course, those with an index of 1 to 14. If you achieved a gross score of 86 on this course, you have scored net par, which should always be your aim.

the stroke index will help you to improve your game just by planning better.

I can give you a little example of this. On a par-4 hole measuring 400 yards you would need a good tee-shot of well over 200 yards and a long iron or fairway wood hit very accurately to the green to set up a par. A medium to high handicap

The 18th at The Belfry, clearly showing how dangerous the second shot could be for any golfer attempting to reach the green. The safe shot is to lay up short.

golfer would find this fairly difficult, at least on a consistent basis. Yet most golfers are quite capable of hitting a 5-iron about 150 yards reasonably straight.

Yet if the hole is 400 yards long the chances are the stroke index will give you an extra shot, so you have three shots to reach the green and two putts for a five, which with the stroke received, is a net par. The sensible option would be to hit a 5-iron from the tee, another 5-iron and then a short iron to the green. Sadly, not very many golfers would consider hitting

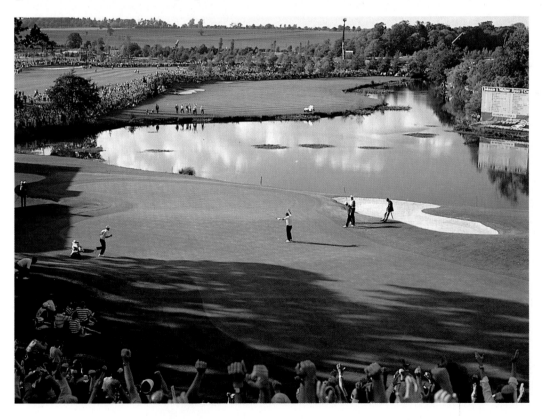

a 5-iron from the tee, particularly with a 400-yard fairway stretching out in front of them. Most would reach for the driver or 3-wood.

Yet you can see that the 5-iron, or maybe the 5-wood for a little more distance off the tee combined with accuracy, could easily be the most sensible choice you have.

When you are ready for your approach shot you need to look carefully at the pin position as well as the location of any bunkers there are around the green. The object is to land the ball safely on the green so that your next stroke is a putt rather than a bunker shot.

This may mean aiming away from the pin itself, as we did some time ago when we had a difficult bunker shot. The hole is not always cut in a "friendly" position so if you aim directly at it you could well be playing straight into some trouble. If the hole is cut on the "fat" part of the green you have the option of playing straight at it, but if it is not, your safer shot could be to the middle, or heart of the green. That may leave you a longer putt but it does mean that you are on the green rather than either just off the green or in the bunker.

You should think about your strategy when you are on the green itself. From the section on putting

Above: On a long putt try to imagine a circle around the hole and aim to get inside that rather than in the hole itself.

Below: It is often the sensible option to play to the fat part of the green, rather than going directly at the pin.

we saw the futility of leaving a putt short; the object is to hole it, and unless it has enough speed the ball will not reach the hole. Yet there are certain long putts where your only realistic aim is to get the ball close enough to the hole to make sure that you hole out with the next stroke. In these circumstances you should imagine a two-foot circle around the hole; your aim is to get the ball to finish inside the circle. Concentrating on this larger, imaginary circle is much easier than trying to concentrate on the very tiny hole itself.

On a long putt, ask your partner to tend the flag for you. Having your partner standing by the hole helps to put the distance into better perspective.

Strokeplay

Years ago most golf was played on the matchplay format, where each hole is a separate challenge. If you took a very high score on one hole you probably only lost that hole rather than ruining your entire round.

Things have changed now and the majority of major tournaments and many club competitions are played on the strokeplay formula, where every shot really does count towards your final score.

The problem with strokeplay is that you can not afford to have one very bad hole with a double or triple bogey. Planning your round thus becomes a little more important but if you approach it in a professional frame of mind you will be on the road to success.

No professional gets to the first tee without a game plan. Not one of them just turns up with the intention of doing his best. There is more to it than that. Every tournament player will have an idea of what score he or she wants to return. The difficulty of the course and the weather conditions will have an effect on their aims, which tend to be realistic.

The first thing a professional looks at is the number of par-5s on the course, knowing that, in most cases, his extra power will allow him to reach the green in two, setting up a possible birdie putt, or even an eagle.

The first part of the strategy is in place, to save maybe three shots on the par-5s. A look at the length of the par-4s will also reveal a birdie opportunity or two, and he will be hoping to get close enough to single putt on at least one par-3.

So, before he starts from the first tee he knows that he is looking to save maybe six shots. Realistically, he will also be aware that he might drop one or two on difficult holes and these will be taken into account.

Most professionals plan their round three holes at a time, having in mind that they will, for example, par the first and second and get a birdie on the third.

They will then move their minds on to the fourth, fifth and sixth and so on. Planning too far ahead is distracting yet, as I mentioned earlier, you must have a game plan that relates to real potential, rather than just hoping.

In strokeplay every single shot counts so you must maintain a high level of concentration throughout the round.

Many club players start off slowly, often because they have failed to warm up and hit a few dozen golf balls on the practice ground first. Then, as they get into the swing of things their scores pick up.

The dropped shots at the start of the round could be saved by warming up and hitting some shots on the practice ground first, though every player, from those just beginning to the Open champion, suffers first tee nerves.

There is no way to stop these, but you can control them by controlling your first shot. Whilst a professional may well reach for the driver on the first tee the

Many par-3 holes have a "bail-out" area to one side. If you doubt your ability, use your common sense.

club golfer might be advised to be less ambitious and to hit a shorter club.

If you are proficient with the 3-wood use that; if not try the 5-wood. You should even consider hitting something really simple, like a 5-iron, from the first tee if you are nervous, just to get the ball in play and away from any other players who might be waiting or watching near the first tee, particularly at busy times.

The aim on the first tee is to get the ball safely in the fairway. Don't worry too much about distance and don't let any playing partners push you into hitting a shot you don't want to.

You should make up your mind what shot you are going to play before you step up to the ball. If your partner stands there with a driver and you are thinking 5-wood, then play the 5-wood, but do so positively. Never address the ball if you are wondering whether you are doing the right thing.

The same goes anywhere on the course; never change your mind halfway through a shot or you will, almost inevitably, make a hash of it.

You won't often have the chance of a caddy to help you judge distances to the green but you can help yourself by using one of the course planners if available. These give you the distances to the front of the green, and to and from important landmarks, such as bunkers. At all times, play your round sensibly.

Matchplay

Matchplay is different and, to many, far more a test of golf than strokeplay, as it puts two players directly against one another.

The advantage of matchplay is that, if you do make a real mess of one hole, taking two or more shots over par, you have not affected your entire round, but just the outcome on that hole.

The first few holes in matchplay can be important and, whilst you should never take too many risks early on, you should be aiming to win the first hole. This need not mean having to hit a 240-yard drive, though; it means getting the first tee shot into the fairway safely so that you can hit your second onto the green or short of any trouble which may surround the putting surface. Trying to do too much on that first hole may well result either in a poor drive, possibly into the rough, or having the second shot miss the green and leave you with a bunker shot.

Giving yourself too much pressure early on is not good course management. in matchplay or strokeplay.

In matchplay, though, it is your opponent you are playing and if he or she hits a superb first drive followed by an approach shot to within inches of the pin, you will have no option but to attack.

Be careful, however, that you continue to play sensibly and within your limits.

As the game progresses you need to be able to weigh up how your opponent is playing and where he or she is at their most vulnerable. It might be on short shots, it might be on the green or it may be on par-3s, for example. In those

If your opponent is unhappy on the tee of par-3s, aim your shot at the heart of the green. Put him under pressure.

instances you should attack, giving extra concentration to your shots in an attempt to win those holes.

Obviously, as the game goes on you will either get yourself into a winning position or need to win a few holes to avoid defeat. In those instances you have little option but to attack, but do plan your way carefully rather than just hitting and hoping. Always play the shots you know you can play regularly, rather than the once-in-a-lifetime shot.

Finally, a word on conceding putts, which you are allowed to do in match-play. Many professionals suggest that, if you have safely holed out and cannot lose the hole, you concede a putt or two early in the round to subliminally suggest to your opponent that every short putt will be conceded. Then, when he or she is looking for a concession later, you ask them to hole out.

You should, however, never concede a putt that can beat you by a single stroke, nor any putts that could give your opponent a birdie as that will just further boost their confidence.

A word of warning, finally. Never expect to be given a putt, nor pick the ball up unless you are certain your opponent has conceded your putt; and never putt the ball once your putt has been conceded by your opponent. Just pick the ball up and move your mind to the next hole.

Concentration

Golf is a very disjointed game, a round often taking up to (and sometimes more than) four hours, yet the time actually swinging the golf club is less than two minutes per round.

The average swing, from start to finish, takes just over one second. Even with the time addressing the ball, getting your alignment correct, taking a couple of practice swings and preparing to swing the club probably takes not much more than thirty seconds. That makes something like forty minutes of "real" golf in a four hour round.

Keeping your concentration for the entire four hours is not possible, yet you need to be totally focused for those thirty seconds or so once you reach your ball and prepare to play the shot.

Many professionals these days visit sports psychiatrists to learn how to switch their concentration on and off. For the average golfer that is not an option that can be seriously considered.

What you should do prior to each shot, though, is to turn off all extraneous thoughts and think only of the shot facing you. Forget any bad shots earlier in the round or on this hole in previous games and go back to the basics. Ensure your alignment and set up are correct and just concentrate on swinging smoothly.

Take a couple of deep breaths before you take your shot and slow down as much as you can. If anything distracts you, walk away from the ball and start all over again.

We have mentioned earlier about first tee nerves and how to control them by just hitting a medium iron or 5-wood safely down the middle of the fairway, but quite often, out on the course, players get flustered if they feel they are holding up a group behind. If you feel pressured by their presence behind you, stand aside and call them through. It's better to have them out of the way rather than continually having to look over your shoulder.

You cannot, of course, let every group through as if the course is very busy you could end up standing there all day, which is not a sensible option. All you can do is to try to ignore any players behind you. Get to your ball faster but then take longer playing your shot by really concentrating on your alignment, grip and the swing. In such circumstances you will often try to rush your shot, but that will, in the long run, cause you to take even more time as you may well hit a few shots that are not quite straight, and have to spend time searching for the ball.

In every case where you feel under pressure, for any reason, *slow down.*

Equipment

choosing it and caring for it

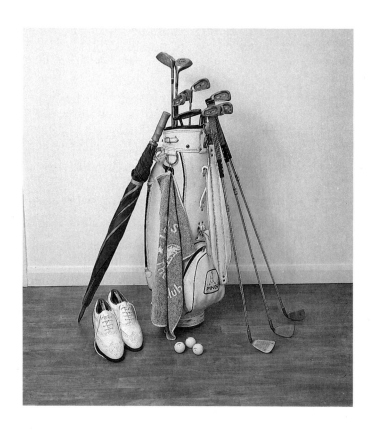

Choosing equipment

Choosing a set of golf clubs is not easy. There are, on the market, a vast number of different makes and styles. Getting the clubs that suit you and your game will take some time and effort, but it is time worth taking rather than just buying the first set the salesman tries to sell you.

There are two main types of club in use at the moment, blades and cavity backed (or peripherally weighted) clubs. Blades are more often used by better players and professionals as they tend to be forged and are thus softer than the cavity-backed clubs which tend to be cast.

However, many profes-

sionals are now using the cavity backed clubs. These were designed with a bigger "sweet spot" which gives the less experienced player a better opportunity to hit the ball straight, as well as to get it airborne, the cavity backed clubs having heavier heads than traditional blades. The weights around their periphery also help to bring the club head back square to the ball as they are being swung.

Certainly they tend to give the less accomplished player more confidence by getting the ball airborne much faster, unlike a blade which needs to be swung well if it is to hit the ball straight and high.

Club manufacturers also make different types of shaft and these can affect your

The main difference between a cavity-backed club and a blade can be seen in this picture. The cavity backed club has more weight in the head and therefore gets the ball airborne better, whilst the peripheral weighting helps to keep it square to the target chosen at address.

Graphite clubs should be kept in a specially constructed bag which has extra padding to protect the shafts.

game. The most popularly used material for shafts is steel, but this can come in varying degrees of stiffness. A stiff shaft is better for the better player whilst a more flexible version is ideal for those who lack distance in their shots.

Graphite, too, can be an advantage for the shorter hitter, and particularly for women, because it is light and flexible, allowing the player to produce more power at impact with the same swing.

Space does not permit a thorough examination of all club and shaft types and flexes, but you should try out several different styles of club before buying a set. Never just go for a set of clubs because they look good. Always try the clubs out. Most professionals and the majority of golf superstores have a small selection of trial clubs which they are only too happy to let you try. Take advantage of this opportunity.

Once you have bought them you must look after them. Head covers are vital for

Clean the grooves after every game and always wipe any grass off the face before you play each shot.

most drivers and for forged blades, as they can be easily damaged. For graphite shafts you are well advised to buy a bag with special padding to protect the shafts.

When you finish playing clean the clubs, wiping any mud or grass from the grooves. Incidentally, on the course, you should always wipe any grass from the club face before you take a shot, and particularly if you have had a practice swing or two. You are bound to have some grass on the face and this will lessen the contact between club and ball, adversely affecting the shot.

Shoes should be kept clean and dry at all times if they are to last and to remain relatively waterproof.

Always hang your rainproof clothing up in a dry, airy room. Leaving it rolled up in the golf bag or the car will result in the rainproof qualities deteriorating rapidly. Some modern rainwear can be machine washed, but check the labels carefully.

Finally, look after your shoes and your clothing, particularly rainproofs. Never leave it rolled up in your golf bag or in the back of the car. It needs to be hung up in a warm room to dry out thoroughly.

If not it will soon lose its rainproof qualities.

Golf equipment is expensive. Treat it well and it will treat you well.

Practice routines

Practice routines

Nobody can achieve a high level of competence at anything unless they practise, be it pianist, artist, dancer or sportsman. Golf is no different. Although reading this book, and referring to it often, will help you to understand the game better, it is no substitute for practice.

Yet many club golfers go from week to week without hitting a single practice shot. They then wonder why, at the weekend, they play so poorly, often missing simple putts and fluffing what should be easy shots. It is safe to say that virtually every golfer would improve if he or she practised on a regular basis.

As a European Tour player I'm lucky. The European Tour venues all provide excellent facilities on a week to week basis and I also have first class practice facilities at my home club of Minchinhampton in Gloucestershire when I am not away on the Tour. It's easy for me to tell you to practise when so many clubs and courses lack even basic practice facilities and your hardest job is to find somewhere suitable to practise, but if you seriously want to improve your golf you will have to spend some time practising.

On the practice ground start with the short clubs and work up to the driver; never start hitting long shots until you have warmed up properly.

You don't have to hit balls eight hours a day seven days a week to improve your golf. Few people would have the time to do that; but chipping in your garden or putting indoors on the carpet will help you enormously, for it is often in the short game and on the greens that the average golfer could improve his or her score most rapidly.

When you do practise it is advisable to

work on your game constructively, rather than just going to the driving range and hitting golf balls without any real plan or purpose. By this I mean that you would be better hitting fifty balls with 100% concentration rather than a hundred balls with only 50% concentration.

Particularly in the winter months when you may spend more time at a covered

Use extra clubs on the ground to help you with your alignment on the practice ground. It helps to train your eyes to get the alignment correct when you are on the course itself.

golf driving range than on a golf course, you can still practise constructively. You should warm up properly, and possibly more so as the weather is likely to be cold.

Begin with the short shots, hitting something like a 9-iron to one of the targets that there are on the driving range; never just hit the ball without a definable target. As you warm up and get the swing rhythm going, try hitting shots on an imaginary golf course, using a course you know as your model. Your local course may have a 350 yard par-4 to begin, so imagine that you are aiming down the first fairway with a driver. If you hit that well and believe you have just 120 yards to go to the pin, use your 8-iron or whatever, again to a real target and see how close you can land it.

During a session at a driving range you will probably wish to work on one aspect of your game and you should do that, but do introduce some novel and alternative ideas for two reasons.

Firstly, it stops you from getting bored; and secondly it will help you measure your ability. After all, if you hit fifty shots with a 5-iron, the chances are that you will hit some of them very well. But on the course you only have one chance to hit a good shot, so using this little exercise at a driving range will help you to judge your progress.

When you are back on the golf course you would be better to take a little longer over each shot and get it right.

I realise that not everyone has sufficient time to practise but if you want to improve your golf you must find some time in each week to work on some part of your game.

So often you hear club golfers coming into the professional shop before they play complaining about aches and pains. Some of them say, quite correctly, that they are going to hit some balls to warm up before playing, yet that good intention could do them more harm because of the way they "warm up".

The problem is that they often go straight to the practice ground, take out a club, normally the driver or 3-wood, and begin hitting balls. You can see the same thing at every driving range in the world. To anyone with any aches or pains, or anyone past the first flush of youth where the body is in prime condition (or should be), doing that could be dangerous.

What I recommend, and do myself on a regular basis is a series of easy stretching exercises. I actually do these when I first get up every morning, gently stretching the body's long muscles, those in the arms, legs and back. I must stress that this needs to be gentle; you should never try to jerk or over-stretch muscles that are cold, particularly just after you get out of bed in the morning. You would be better advised to do so after a hot shower or bath when the muscles have been gently moving a little after a night's sleep.

However, before playing golf, as with any other physical sport, you need to loosen up the main sets of muscles you will be using. Basically these are the large sets of muscles, legs, arms and back, and the wrists and fingers. You can do these exercises either in the changing room or out on the practice ground.

When you have spent about five to ten minutes warming up you are ready to begin hitting some shots, though you should never begin with the driver. Start

Bend and stretch to loosen all your main golfing muscles; turning exercises like these can also help you improve your swing.

at the opposite end of the bag, with the sand wedge or wedge, hitting a dozen shots with that to get the swing going. Always aim at a specific target rather than just hitting golf balls aimlessly into the far distance.

On the practice ground I always lay a couple of clubs down to give me the ball-to-target line and the parallel line for my feet. It's the only time in golf you can do this, so use the opportunity. If you can guarantee that you are standing correctly aligned on the practice ground it will help your eyes to see that you are standing correctly out on the course, when you can't use other clubs to align yourself. Make golf easier.

You might not have the time to work completely through the bag, which is probably not necessary anyway, at least just for a warming-up session. Hit six to eight shots with, say, the sand wedge, 9-iron, 7-iron, 5-iron and 3-iron, then a dozen with the 3- or 5-wood, then the same with the driver. On every shot, line up, get your grip right, check your stance and hit the ball to a specific target. There are often a few flags planted at various distances on the practice ground. You

Even though you may not have the time or money to have regular lessons you should have an occasional lesson from your golf professional.

should be trying to get the ball to land right by them, using whichever club you think necessary.

When you reach the driver have a specific target in mind and try to shape the shot to whatever is your normal pattern. If, for example, you are an habitual fader of the ball, aim slightly left so that the ball comes round to land in the correct position. If you can shape your shots at will,

On the practice ground take the time to recheck your grip and set up. You must make it a habit if you are to play golf to the best of your ability.

try a few fades, a few draws, a couple of high shots and, if it is windy, a few shots boring under the wind, staying low to their target.

So many players at club level only ever begin hitting decent shots on about the fourth hole; if they had only hit a few practice shots they would have found their swing rhythm before they reached the first tee, not the fifth.

This book will, if you follow the advice given, help you substantially to understand your game, and to have the means to improve it. Every player should, though, at every level, have their own personal coach. Every professional does.

I work regularly with my golf professional who can see me when I swing, something I can't do myself. He understands my game and my swing, having watched it develop over a period of time and he can quickly detect any faults which do, unfortunately but inevitably, creep into my game.

Whilst realising that the average player does not have the time or money to have a lesson with a professional every day, or even every week, you will find regular lessons with one professional most rewarding. It may take a couple of lessons before he (or she, as a growing number of golf professionals are ladies) gets to know your swing and it takes a little while for changes in your swing to work their way through into better on-course results, so don't go looking for a quick fix as it doesn't happen. You need to persevere and you need to practise.

It often helps, if you can't have weekly golf lessons, to practise with a friend who will grow to understand your swing and should be able to detect any major changes in your swing. He or she may well be able to see any faults in your alignment or grip, which you yourself cannot see. Whilst I must warn you against religiously following well meant but unqualified advice, some help is better than none, even if it is only concerned with your alignment. As we have seen earlier in this book, most faults in golf happen before you begin to swing the club.

Finally, a word to those who reach the first tee without having spent 20 or 30 minutes warming up. You can still take a couple of minutes loosening some of the larger muscles, particularly those in your shoulders, back and legs.

From the pictures on the previous page you can see that, even after having had an hour warming up before a tournament round, I still perform some stretching muscles whilst waiting on the first tee to begin my round. This has two main benefits. Firstly it helps to keep the muscles warm and loose, allowing me to swing properly without feeling any tightness in the muscles.

Secondly it helps me to relax as there is always a few minutes' wait before we begin, with the official starter announcing the match number, our names and so on. Taking tension away at this stage is important if I am to get away to a good start on the first tee.

If you want to play golf to the best of your ability you have to adopt a professional attitude, thinking about your shots and about your game. You can't do that if your muscles are tight and cold. Warm up, practise intelligently, and take your time over each shot. You only get the one chance. Good luck.

Take time to practise shots from sloping or difficult lies, too, rather than just hitting from flat surfaces.

Glossary

some frequently used golfing terms

Ace	A hole in one
Birdie	A score of one under par (e.g. 2 on a par-3)
Bogey	A score of one over par (e.g. 5 on a par-4)
Carry	The distance a ball travels in the air before it hits the ground
Chip	A low, running shot to the green
Choke down	Gripping the club further down the handle to give more control
Closed face	When the face of the club is turned to the right of the target
Closed stance	When the feet and body are aligned left of the target
Cocking the wrists	The bending of the wrists as you swing the club back
Cut	A shot which fades from right to left in the air
Divot	A piece of turf which is removed as you hit the ball
Eagle	A score of two under par (e.g. 2 on a par-5)
Handicap	The allowance a player receives against the par of the course
Honour	The player winning the previous hole is allowed to tee off first
Hood	Setting the hands ahead of the ball, thus decreasing the loft
Hook	To move the ball left to right in the air
Open face	When the face of the club is turned to the left of the target
Open stance	When the feet and body are aligned to the right of the target
Par	The standard score for a particular hole
Pin	The flagstick
Pitch	A fairly short shot hit high to the green
Scratch	A handicap of zero
Shank	The hosel of the club, where the shaft and head meet
SSS	Standard Scratch Score for a golf course, based on its length
Stroke index	Relative difficulty of each hole, the easiest being index 18
Tee	The area from which you play the ball at the start of each hole

Special thanks to

Golfs d'Hardelot; Haverhill GC
West Derby GC
Minchinhampton GC
Simon Mayfield; Nick Brace
Peter Dawson; Stuart Little
Tony Thompson; Paul Gardiner